THE NEW MILLENNIUM COLL

ANDALUSIA

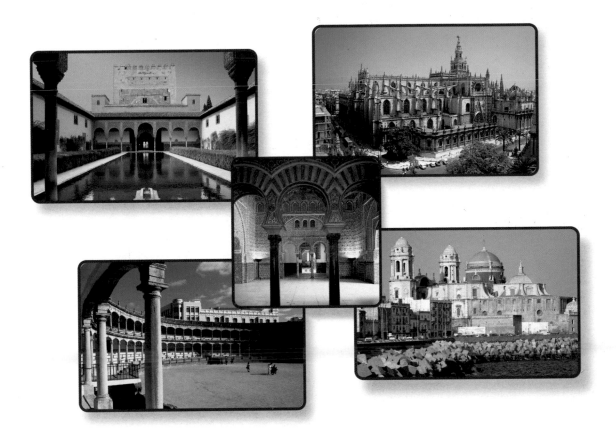

THE INTRIGUING ELEGANCE OF MOORISH ART, THE RHYTHMS OF FLAMENCO AND THE THRILLS OF THE BULLFIGHTS COME TOGETHER IN ONE OF SPAIN'S MOST BEAUTIFUL CITIES

BONECHI

Publication created and designed by Casa Editrice Bonechi
Editorial management: Serena De Leonardis
Cover: Sonia Gottardo. *Editing and make up:* Anna Baldini. *Illustrations:* Stefano Benini
Texts by Carlos Pascual. *Text boxes by* Patrizia Fabbri, *translated by* Shona Cunningham Dryburgh.
Translation: Sonia Ercolini, Julia Weiss (*cover*).

© Copyright by Casa Editrice Bonechi - Firenze - Italia
E-mail: bonechi@bonechi.it - Internet: www.bonechi.it - www.bonechi.com

Printed in Italy by Centro Stampa Editoriale Bonechi.

PHOTOGRAPHY ACKNOWLEDGMENTS
*The majority of the photographs are property of the Casa Editrice Bonechi Archives.
They were taken by* Luigi Di Giovine *(Photographic service),* Marco Bonechi, Paolo Giambone, Andrea Pistolesi.
Other Archives: Gianni Dagli Orti: *page 41 above;* Andrea Pistolesi: *pages 56-57, 118-119;*
Ghigo Roli: *pages 4, 44, 45, 96-97, 105, 108 below, 116-117, 126-127;*
Spanish Tourist Board Office in Rome *(by kind permission): page 114 above and below right* (López Alonso),
page 114 below left (Juan J. Pascal).

The Publisher gratefully acknowledges the Spanish Tourist Board Office in Rome *for its valuable collaboration.*

ISBN 88-476-1141-5

* * *

A picturesque Andalusian village with its whitewashed houses.

INTRODUCTION

When we first mention Andalusia and Andalusians, many people, especially foreigners, immediately think of the pounding of tambourines, the clapping of hands, the cries of Flamenco songs and the lively spirit of the people. They don't have a complete picture of this region.

Andalusia has its own historical character, and the Arab influence, best-known to Europeans, only plays a secondary role in the formation of the region. Andalusia is one of the seventeen autonomous regions of the Spanish State and is also one of the biggest with eight provinces under an autonomous government, the Andalusian Council. For the Spanish people, it is one of the so-called «historical nationalities», that is to say, a region which has fought for its unification and identity for centuries.

This region, which was initially inhabited by thriving kings, mentioned in the Bible, was later invaded by a flow of races who found themselves immersed in its character; the Phoenician dealers with their cargo ships; the intrepid and curious Greeks; a great number of organized and rational Romans who set up the province of Betica; the «Barbarians» of the North who crossed the Straits; the Arabs who later invaded the peninsula turning Andalusia into one of the most thriving and cultured regions in the civilized world of the Middle Ages.

After the Christian conquest, the historical character began to take shape although it was later «discovered» by Saxon adventurers attracted by the Indian epica, others by the political enlightenment, and English traders by its sherry.

One by one, these races made Andalusia part of their people and their world. The Roman influence is just as important as the Arab, Jewish or Christian influences. Its multi-ethnical history corresponds to its contrasting and varied landscape. Andalusia is dominated by the Mediterranean sea which played an important role in this history and culture, linking Oriental and Western Andalusia. Andalusia is made up of the white villages of Ronda, Cazorla, the Sierra Nevada, the Sierra Morena, the sun-bleached deserts of Almería, forming a popular tourist spot and of the farmhouses of the extensive countryside with its marshes full of eucalyptus trees.

Andalusia is enriched by a historical unification of variety and contrast; a world of mythical sea alongside bandits' hide-outs; Moorish arches in the vicinity of Roman columns or Mudejar art; pagan vitality next to adorned Virgins and Christs; the most progressive social restlesness combined with century-old Koranic fatalism.

Andalusia

This is the warm, flourishing land where the River Guadalquivir runs, one of the longest in the country, where golden eagles, pink flamingos, lynx and deer still breed, and where Romans and Moors settled in days gone by, leaving behind their splendid, imposing monuments. In 1492, Christopher Columbus set off from here in search of the dreamed "*buscar el levante por el poniente*". This is the reign of toreros and bullfighting, white beaches and sun-bleached villages, flamenco dancing and *fiestas*; in other words, the very essence and spirit of this sunny Iberian country. And some of the most beautiful cities in Spain, like Cadiz, Cordova, Granada and Malaga, lie between the dazzling sands of the Costa del Sol and the breathtaking beauty of the national parks.

5

◄ *The Door of Justice near the Renaissance fountain called Charles V's Basin.*

The solid mass of the Alhambra is silhouetted against the nearby Sierra mountains.

GRANADA

When the Andalusian poet Manuel Machado tried to describe Granada in only four words, he chose the following: «secret water which cries». The most surprising thing about this Andalusian province, which lies between the highest peaks of the peninsula and the coast, is in fact the proximity of the snow and the sea. It is an amazing fact that in spring the tourists here can ski on the Sierra Nevada slopes in the morning and then lie on the beaches around Motril, Salobreña or Almuñecar in the afternoon. The «secret» water is the soul of Granada as it trickles through the high peaks of the Sierra, feeding its land and re-appearing in abundance in its streams, fountains, and brooks. Granada was the last Arabic redoubt in Spain; at a time when the whole peninsula had been converted back to Christianity, the last Nazarenes accompanied their splendid Baroque architecture with whispering fountains. Granada's soul plays an important role in the architecture of the Naza-

rene palaces and homes just like the titles, marble, plaster, interlacing and arabesque decoration. When the last king of Granada was overthrown and defeated by the Catholic Monarchs in 1491, he fled from the city with tears in his eyes: it wasn't caused by a woman's weakness as legend has it but Granada's soul reflecting in his eyes for the last time.

If the Nazarene influence was generous and powerful for Granada, so was the Christian influence. The immense, lengthy shadow of the Alhambra can't hide the string of towers, convents, palaces and hospitals. The existence of so many different cultural elements has created an open and tolerant yet agonizing Unamuno character in the people of Granada; it is no coincidence that Mariana de Pineda, one of the greatest Spanish women myths, and the liberal tormented Ganivet who committed suicide from Granada, nor that Federico García Lorca was shot in Granada, his home-town.

A view of the Alcazaba,
the oldest part of the Alhambra.

The Alcazaba's strong towers.

LA ALHAMBRA

On top of a steep hill overlooking the city, the Alhambra rises up, facing its sister hill of Albaicín, separated from it by the Darro river, with the snow-tipped peaks of the Sierra Nevada in the background. Known as the Bermejo Castle, which comes from the Arabic word alluding to the red clay used to build its walls, it is the oldest, most impressive and best preserved Arabic palace in the world.

The first Nazarene king, Alhamar, decided to move his court from Albaicín, the main settlement, to the next neighbouring hill in 1238. Alhamar's successors continued to expand the monumental structure. Abu Hachach Yusuf I and his son and heir, Mohamed V, were the instigators of the main transformation and construction in the XIV century, which still exists today. The complex of towers, walls, palaces and gardens was adapted to the land's structure and was in-

spired by the finest oriental spirit. After the Christian conquest in the XV century, it continued to be the royal palace and underwent new constructions and transformations.

After the first ritual ascent of the Cuesta de Gomérez walking through the romantic avenues with their downward flow of fresh, sparkling water, we finally come face to face with one of the richest and most complete monumental complexes. We can begin this visit at the last of Granada's doors (XVI century); on the right the Bermejas towers, erected in the XI or XII century to reinforce the wall, loom up. After crossing the avenue, which can be done by car, we have to go through the Puerta de la Justicia and then through the Puerta del Vino to reach the spacious Plaza de los Algibes; it owes its name to the underground deposits laid down in the XVI century and can be used as a reference point to visit different sectors.

In chronological order, we can begin our visit at the *Alcazaba* which is, as its name indicates, a castle to

The north door of the Mexuar's Patio.

The main hall of the Mexuar, transformed during the XVIIth century into a Christian chapel.

9

◀ *The magnificent ceiling of the
Cuarto Dorado in worked, gilded wood.*

*The Patio of the Myrtles, with the 45 metre high
tower of Comares, the Alhambra's highest construction.*

defend the residential palaces of the Alhambra. Between it and the Alcazaba you will pass through the Adarve garden, a simple garden filled with the scent of box-wood, used in the past as a defense weapon. The most important part of the Alcazaba is the *Torre de la Vela*, thus named as it watched over the city from its strategic position; there the alarm was sounded in times of danger and its bell regulated the irrigation shift.

From the tower we can enjoy and appreciate this une-qualled view. In the distance we can see the snow-tipped peaks of the Sierra and down below the new city spreading out towards the Vega round about the palaces and gardens. In the middle of the Alcazaba we find the Plaza de Armas where we can observe the remains of small military quarters. The Puerta and Torre de Armas overlooks the Albaicín.

After the preliminary visit we can now enter into the intimate world of the residential palaces, where delicate details and refined sensuality contrast with the harsh military enclosure and weapons. Fundamentally, the palace is built around two patios — the Patio de los Arrayanes and the Patio de los Leones. Around the Patio de los Arrayanes all public activities such as public

audiences, meeting and receptions took place. The rooms around the Patio de los Leones where the sultan's private life envolved, have a more intimate and familiar character.

Leaving the Machuca gardens on your left you enter the *Sala del Mexuar* or Sala del Consejo, which under-went the greatest change when Charles V converted it into an oratory in 1629. Nevertheless remains of the original colours of the ornamental tiles and the ara-besque plaster decoration from the times of Mohamed V are still preserved; the interlacing designs of the small chapel at the end of the room have recently been re-stored. With regard to these renovations, it would be useful to consult Gallego Burín's observations in his classical *Artistic and historical guide to the city of Gra-nada*: «despite the present homogeneity of these struc-tures, there are however some essential differences be-tween the later palaces. While on one hand the Coma-res is essentially Muslim, the Leones is characterized by Christian variations and influences, which undoubtedly originate from the relationship between the architect, Mohamed V, and the king of the Castle, Peter I. It's sometimes difficult to explain these differences due to

chronological problems with regard to the Alhambra caused by frequent renovations and numerous restorations carried out since the Catholic Monarchs' reign, first by Mouresque architects whose work was easily confused with past works and later perfected in modern times».

After crossing the Patio del Mexuar, with its marble paving, we arrive at the *Cuarto Dorado*, also called Cuarto del Mexuar, de la Mezquita, and de Comares (the toponymy of the whole Alhambra varies according to guides and causes a great deal of confusion).

The south façade is the most impressive part of the Cuarto Dorado and proves to be one of the most interesting elements in the whole Alhambra with its best Nazarene stuccoes and ornamental tiles.

Finally we come out onto the famous Patio de Comares, best known as the Patio de los Arrayanes or de los Mirtos (*arrayán* is the Arabic equivalent of the Greek-Latin term *myrtle*) or de la Alberca or del Estanque... The **Patio de los Arrayanes** which looks bigger than it really is (36.5 m by 23.5 m) sums up all the equilibrium and serenity of Nazarene architecture even though it has undergone many architectural changes (the rooms in the south gallery were destroyed to fit in the Renaissance Machuca palace). In the XIX century, a family of

architects, José, Rafael and Mariano Contreras carried out so many alterations that rumour has it that the Contreras family were the authentic builders of the Alhambra! Fortunately the last conservationists and restorers erased all traces of these alterations and tried to bring the rooms back to their original form.

The patio is dominated by the powerless presence of the **Torre de Comares** which is part of the walled enclosure. It is sombre and threatening with its embrasures, battlements and huge structure, emphasizing the public and official nature of this section. An elegant door delicately reflected in the surface of the pool gives access to the **Sala de la Barca** which is not named after the keel shape cedar panelling but derives from the Arabic word *baraka* meaning blessing or look. The room's ceiling burnt down in a fire in 1890 and had to be completely rebuilt. It was used as the anteroom for the **Salon de Embajadores**, the biggest in the palace; it served as a throne room where the Sultan received foreign emissaries. This square-shaped room is more than eleven metres long and almost twenty metres high. Each side of the room looks out onto three balconies; there is a twin centre balcony, and above it, windows with wooden shutters dominated by linear and graphic forms let the light filter through.

Three pictures of the Sala de los Embajadores, with its rich marble decorations and azulejos.

Two pictures of the Lions Patio, which is so famous that it has become the Alhambra's symbol.

On the next two pages, yet another two details of the Lions' Patio.

From these balconies we can enjoy the best view over the avenue which goes down towards the Darro River. The decoration is a prodigy of finely entwining strands of plasterwork which has a hypnotic effect on whoever looks at it. According to tradition, the signing of the surrender pact of the city by the Moorish King Boadbil El Chico to the Catholic Monarchs took place in this room. Another legend affirms that Queen Isabel offered her jewels to Columbus here to finance his journey to the unknown. Not to mention other stories and legends about Boabdil and his mother...

Returning to the Patio de los Arrayanes, in front of us stands another twin door which is reflected on the opposite side of the pool. The room above is said to have housed the Monarch's *harem*.

On the opposite side of the Patio de los Arrayanes, there is a small slope which leads us into the most intimate and private sector of the palace. The **Patio de los Leones** is a magnificent man-made oasis which opens out into different rooms. The fine white marble columns spread out like graceful palm trees and lead towards the centre fountain filled with sparkling water which reflects the light and illuminates the dark rooms. There are 124 columns, some in groups of two, three or four as in the pavillions. Despite their elegant and stylish similarity, they are in fact all different. The pavillions' interlacing patterns are a splendid example of carpentry and with the columns give rise to a palm-tree, oasis effect, perhaps the only prevailing image in one of the smallest yet best-known patios in the world (28×15 metres, only 441 square metres).

The twelve archaic, stylized lions which carry a cup on their backs, are of more recent (XVI century) but the cup itself is a splendid piece dating back to centuries before. On the brim, there is a part of the *inscription* dedicated by the poet Zemreo to Mohamed V engraved in the marble; amongst other things it asks: «Is it by chance that this garden offers us a work whose beauty is to remain unique in the eyes of God?». The fountain's primitive appearance has been covered up, like the oriental pavillion, since a second cup was added to the fountain in the XVII century, and a third one in 1838, and the pavillion was covered with a strange dome. Coming out of the harem, after intruding on the Sul-

◄ *The dome with stalactites*
in the Sala de las dos Hermanas.

A detail of the decoration of the
Sala de las dos Hermanas, one of the
palace's most sumptuous rooms.

tan's private quarters, we find on the west-side the **Sala de los Mocárabes**, named after the work on its ceiling, although it was destroyed in an explosion in 1590 and rebuilt in the XVII century (today we can see part of the early and new section). A patio opens up through three archways.

On the right side, the **Sala de los Abencerrajes** broods in its sombre memories: according to a dubious legend, the monarch, uncertain whether it was Mohamed, Muley, Hacen, or Boabdil, ordered the beheading of the famous high class nobles of the Abencerrajes; according to tradition, the rusty-red marks on the marble of the fountain were caused by the blood of the defeated warriors who were sacrificed one by one as they entered the room.

On the side opposite the Sala de los Mocárabes: the **Sala de los Reyes** or Sala del Tribunal, or de la Justicia.

It is divided into sections corresponding to the three arches at the entrance forming dome-covered sections with arch windows at the starting-points.

At the end of the room, bedrooms open up to us containing the most curious decorations of the whole section: leather paintings which line the wooden dome. They are not top quality but are interesting because of the lack of representational art in the whole Alhambra enclosure. According to Gallego Burín «much has been said about these paintings which are undoubtebly Christian». In fact, they date back to the XIV century and were probably painted by Christian artists from Seville: some critics dare to say that the artist was of Tuscan origin or training due to the Italian style of these oil paintings of sultans and their ancestors.

Finally, on the other side, we come to one of the most beautiful Baroque rooms in the Alhambra, the **Sala de**

The exquisite Mirador de Daraxa (or Lindaraja)
with its beautiful stuccowork
on the walls similar to inlaid ivory.

The small, poetic Lindaraja Garden
seen from above.

las dos Hermanas, named after the two great white marble sister flagstones in the middle of the room acting as a background for the indoor fountain. The rooms seemingly formed the living quarters of the sultan and his family, and here his sons' official brides were confined if renounced by the monarchy. The tiled panelling, the colours of the plaster, and the dome's interlacing turn this room into a rich, extravagant jewel. The room, built during the last days of the reign of Mohamed V, reveals two small rooms at the side, one called the **Sala de los Ajimeces**, thus named because of the twin balconies which look onto the garden (they aren't exactly «ajimeces» because the ajimez is a raised, enclosed balcony with shutters), is covered with a precious roof probably built in a later period (XVI century).

The **Mirador de Daraja** or Daraxa is named after the Arab expression «i'ain dar aixa» which means «the eyes of the sultan's house»; however according to one of the many legends about the palace, the name comes from Lindaraja, the daughter of the governor of Malaga for whom this extravagant romantic fantasy was supposedly built.

It is even more beautiful if we remember that it was built with plain and simple materials like plaster, tiles, ceramic... and also with elements like light, shadows, water, landscape and above all with imagination. On the walls is an inscription contemplating the immense beauty: «I have brought together such beauty that the stars in the heavenly skys are lit up by it»; in another line which maybe alludes to the magic of some of the ephemeral elements: «when one contemplates my beauty he is deluded with outward appearance».

At the intersection of the two main sections of the Alhambra, the Comares palace and El Cuarto de los Leones, we discover the *Hamman* or **Sala de Baños**, on a different level. To reach them go down the Patio de la Reja or de los Cipreses, after crossing Charles V's rooms.

The rooms were built at the time when the emperor intended to make Granada the capital of his kingdom, but he never used them. On the other hand, the North American writer, Washington Irving, used four of these rooms as a setting for his romantic «Tales of the Alhambra» in 1829. In 1959 to commemorate his centenary, some of the romantic scenes were acted out here. The rooms were built over the garden and on the «Torre de Abul Hachach» wall converting it and its tower to the **Galeria del Tocador** and **Tocador de la Reina** for the

The beautiful perspective of the Sala de los Reyes, or Hall of Justice.

One of the frescoes that decorate the ceiling of the Sala de los Reyes with the dazzling colours of a Persian miniature.

An overview of the white houses
of the Albaicín from one of
the numerous miradores.

The "resting room" in the royal bathrooms, ▶
with four columns supporting the central
part and a fine decoration of majolicas forming
a mosaic in the niches which open on the walls.

empress Isabel, Charles V's ill-fated wife. The Peinador and Gallery are in fact two good balconies which decorate the tower, painted by two of Raphael's disciples, Julio Aquiles and Alejandro Mayner.

The baths which date back to the time of Yusuf, underwent some dubious «restorations» in the XIX century (carried out by Contreras). We first enter the Sala de las Camas from where the king could look at the women coming out of the baths and then throw an apple to the one he desired.

The actual bath room quarters feature simple architecture, only decorated with ornamental tiles and which ironically have suffered little changes.

The **Jardín de Lindaraja**, or de Daraxa or de los Naranjos or de los Mármoles, is connected to the baths. It was built by Charles V's architects and was made to replace a terrace or garden at the far end of the Mirador de las dos Hermanas. A Mouresque fountain prevails in this dark and silent corner; its basin was brought here from Mexuar and placed on top of a wooden shaft inside another Renaissance basin. On the brim of the basin we can read the poem written in the memory of Ben Nasar: «I am a great ocean with elegant marble shores and my pearly-white sea spreads out over a finely engraved surface».

From the Jardín de Lindaraja we can begin an interesting tour of the walls and towers which enclose the palace up to the Puerta de la Justicia from where we entered. First of all we cross the **Jardínes del Partal** built in a later period, over the military and servants' quarters

In these four pictures, the Gardens of the Partal, ▶ with its five arches thate are reflected in the quiet waters of the basin. The inlaid wooden ceiling inside the Partal is worth looking at.

and its gardens. We find the Torre de las Damas, which seems to rest beside a peaceful pool, that reveals a richly carved gateway, *partal* meaning gateway. The lions which stand guard on the edge of the pool were brought here in 1843 when the asylum was demolished; it is an institution which proves how the Moslems in Granada were more civilised and rational than the Christians in the rest of Spain, who still believed madness to be an act of the devil. Behind the palm trees reflected in the pool stand three dwelling quarters of the Yusuf period; one of them houses some of the most interesting Mouresque paintings which were discovered in 1907 and prove to be unique in Muslem Spain. These paintings contradict the harsh theory that the Koran clearly prohibited the paintings of live human beings. The hunting scenes and fantastic animals, alongside musicians, singers and warriors are closely related to

the Persian manuscripts of the XIII century. Further on, beside the Torre del Mihrab, there is a small mosque of the Yusuf I period which defends the Puerta de Hierro, the Torre del Cadí and the Torre de la Cautiva, decorated during the Yusuf period and where, according to legend, Lady Isabel de Solís, the favourite Christian character of Muley Halen, was kept prisoner: there is an important inscription in the plaster «stop and observe how each figure delicately follows the next». The Torre de las Infantas follows, in memory of the legendary Zaida, Zoraida and Zorahaida created by Washington Irving, already showing signs of the decadence of Nazarene art.

It is important to remember that even after the Christian conquest the Alhambra was still used as the royal palace. Therefore the presence of the Christian monarchs can still be felt in this great monument.

The solid façade of Charles V's palace and the vast circular courtyard inside it, with the doric columns of the lower open gallery and the ionic columns of the upper one.

THE PALACE OF CHARLES V

Pedro Machuca began building the palace in 1526 in an Italian Renaissance style popular at the time. After his death in 1550, his son Luis continued his work until it was discontinued in the XVII century leaving the palace incomplete; General Franco then ordered the completion of the palace.

It is an atypical structure built according to Spanish tradition, and it emphasizes the strong Italian influence of the time. «It is one of the noblest architectural creations of the Renaissance period and may be one of the most beautiful examples outside Italy», according to Gallego Burín. Despite popular opinion, Machuca did not destroy any Arab structures but made use of the Moslem *randa* or royal cemetary. It rests on doric columns downstairs and ionic columns above. Passing through the Plaza de los Aljibes and the Puerta de la Justicia, we come across two beautiful doorways: the first one is decorated with reliefs by Juan de Orea and Antonio de Leval in the lower part and Juan de Misares in the upper part, and the second one with sculptures by Nicolao de Corte. In the nearest corner to the Patio de los Arrayanes stands an octagonal chapel left incomplete because of the projecting dome.

The palace holds the *Museo de Arte Hispanomusulman* and the *Museo de Bellas Artes*. The first contains a collection of capitals, arabesque plasterwork, wooden carvings, ceramics and various relics found during the excavations carried out in the Alhambra. One of the most outstanding pieces is the «*Alhambra vase*» one of the best and rarest examples of Hispanoarabic ceramics of the XIV century, decorated and engraved in blue and gold on a white background.

The Museo de Bellas Artes houses a rich collection of

A partial view of the hall dedicated to the artist Pedro Anastasio Bocanegra, with the story of the Virgin Mary.

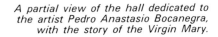

The magnificent sculpture to be found ad the entry to the Fine Arts Museum.

The hall of the Italian fireplace, with the XVIth century fireplace in the wall in the background.

A partial view of the hall dedicated to the artist Sanchez Cotán, and the hall dedicated to Alonso Cano, XVIIth century artist and leading representative of the Granada school. ▶

impressive paintings and sculptures by local artists.

Two of the most outstanding artists come from the school of Granada. Juan Sanchez Cotán (1560-1627), originally from the province of Toledo, became Carthusian in 1603 and lived in the Carthusian monastery in Granada until his death, painting pictures for the refectory and cells of the monastery. His strange darkness must have inspired Zurbarán, who shares the honour of being one of the most talented still-life artists in Spain, a simple, plain style which contrasts with the exuberant and free still-life which was popular at the time in Italian and Flemish art.

Another great artist from Granada is Alonso Cano (1601-1667) who occupies an entire room in the museum.

He was an architect, painter and sculptor who worked in Seville and in the Madrid court, appointed by the Conde-Duque de Olivares. After losing his second wife, who was assassinated under mysterious circumstances in 1664, he retired to the Carthusian mon-

astery in Valencia of Porta Coeli and ended his days in solitude and poverty. His strong character is personified in his works, and while his dark paintings were highly praised by his contemporaries, he went against the popular and affluent Italian and Flemish styles.

There are also some good examples of the work of other Spanish artists and sculptors, for example, Roberto Alemán, Iacopo L'Indaco, Diego de Siloé, Juan de Maeda, Juan de Orea and Vicente Carducho, an Italian emigrant in Spain and a follower of Sanchez Cotán; Pedro de Moya, who has a room dedicated to him, paints with a subtle sensitivity and was influenced by Alonso Cano. Pedro de Mena is also represented with four great paintings which he completed in collaboration with Cano, which we can see in a room dedicated to him. In the **Salón de la Chimenea Italiana**, named after the multicoloured marble XVI century fireplace which was bought in Genoa in 1546 to decorate the palace, XVI and XVII century paintings, tapestries, pieces of furniture and armour are exhibited.

Three pictures of the Generalife Gardens, with
the narrow canal flanked by jets of water,
rose-bushes, orange trees and cypresses:
an oasis of quiet, peace and silence.

JARDINES DEL GENERALIFE

These gardens dominate the Alhambra complex; the
word 'generalife' means either 'raised garden or divine
garden' or 'garden of the architect *Genna-Alarif*'. The
gardens were used at recreation times by the Nazarene
royal family. From the simple architectural structures
we can enjoy an extensive view of the city and La Vega
with the Alhambra in the foureground. We are not in-
terested in the architecture but mainly in the gardens
themselves which embrace the delicate and sensitive
style described by a famous Andalusian composer, Manuel de Falla, in his «Nights in the Spanish gardens».
Every summer, sessions of the classic International
Music and Dance Festival are performed on this splendid, natural stage surrounded by cypress trees.

The Cathedral's façade, which Alonso Cano erected partially changing the original project by Diego de Siloé.

A view of the Cathedral's apse.

The lavishly decorated setting of the Golden ▶
Chapel inside the Cathedral.

THE CATHEDRAL

The Christian conquest of the Arabs affected the spirit at the time in the same way as the contemporary adventure of the discovery of new lands. Therefore we can understand why the Catholic Monarchs, who had completed the historical unification and laid down the foundation of a modern state now open to the discovery of a new world, symbolically chose Granada as their base.

Following their example, families and Christian institutions filled Granada with splendid monuments which

33

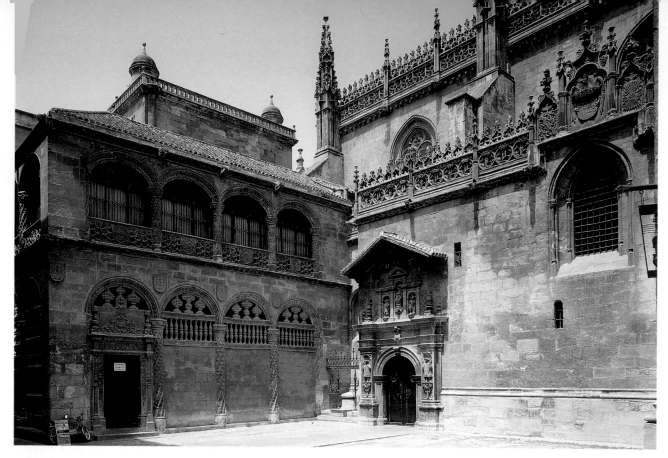

The external access to the Gothic Royal Chapel,
which houses the mortal remains of Ferdinand and Isabelle.

The two Catholic Kings and, under the crypt, the ▶
simple royal sarcophagi.

are only surpassed by the presence of the Alhambra.

The most famous Christian nucleus is clearly the Cathedral with the Royal Chapel used as the Monarchs' mausoleum, the Sagrario, the Lonja de Mercaderes and other buildings like the Palacio Arzobispal, the Palacio de la Madraza or Cabildo Antiguo etc. Enrique de Egas began building the cathedral in a Gothic style in 1523 but Diego de Siloé continued his work in a Renaissance style with five spacious naves. It was consecrated in 1561 but the work continued until 1703. The façade was designed by Alonso Cano and enriched with reliefs by J. Risueño and L. Verdiguier in the XVIII century. The most outstanding doors are the San Jerónimo door by Siloé and that of the ecclesiastic school which features bas-reliefs also by Siloé.

The **Capilla Mayor** is the most beatiful chapel in Spain with statues by Alonso de Mena of the *apostles* and *statues of the Catholic Monarchs praying* by Pedro de Mena as well as paintings by Juan de Sevilla, Bocanegra, and Alonso Cano. The stained-glass windows on the dome are attributed to Juan del Campo according to a Siloé design. The organs are XVIII century and the altar paintings are by Juan de Sevilla and Bocanegra. There are many pieces in the cathedral and its chapels which are worth pointing out, thanks to famous artists like Alonso Cano, Ribera, Martinel Montañes... although the most precious jewel is still the Capilla Real.

Built in a flowery Gothic style by Enrique de Egas between 1505 and 1507 to house the remains of the Catholic Monarchs, who were buried there in 1521, the

Behind the magnificent wrought-iron grates,
the mausoleum of the Catholic Monarchs Ferdinand
and Isabelle, sculptured by the Florentine
Domenico Fancelli in Carrara marble. Alongside
are the tombs of Philip the Handsome
and Joan the Mad by B. Ordóñez.

The interior of the Sacresty, ▶
a real museum of Flemish painting.

Maestro de la Sangre: Pietà. ▶

Capilla Real is enclosed by a railing which is a splendid piece of craftmanship, by Bartolomé de Jaén (1518). *The Monarchs' Tomb* in Carrara Marble is a work of art by Domenico Fancelli. Later the remains of the monarch's daughter, Juana de la Loca, and her unfortunate husband Felipe el Hermoso were brought there and laid in a tomb by Bartolomé Ordoněz (1526). Iacopo l'Indaco's altarpiece dominates the high altar with sculptures by Felipe de Borgoña and reliefs describing the conquest of Granada and the mass conversion of the Moors. In the transept is to be found the *altar's shrine* by Alonso de Mena (1632). On the left, we can admire an outstanding piece by Dierik Bouts, a colourful *trip-*

tych with figurines constituting one of his best works of art. Below, in the crypt, lie lead sarcophagi which were ransacked and emptied during the war against Napoleon's soldiers.

The Royal Chapel's **Sacristy** was built in elegant Renaissance style between 1705 and 1750. Of its contents, the Renaissance font by Francesco l'Indaco is worth pointing out.

The **Lonja de Mercaderes** beside the Royal Chapel is silver-plated and was built in 1518 by Juan Garcia de Prades. In the Palacio de la Madraza, once an old Arab university (its name is a derivation of «Medersa»), Granada's first town council was set up.

Gypsy Granada

The Spanish Gypsies probably came from Africa and arrived in the peninsula in mediaeval times, bringing with them a culture bearing distinct signs of the Indian origin of this people. Over the ages, their traditions, dances and melodies gradually blended with those of passionate Andalusia (an example is the influence on the flamenco), the region where many of them stayed.

Female gypsies and, on the left, the famous Cueva Zambra de la Rojo, in the heart of the Albaicín area.

There is still a large group of gypsies in Granada, where they live in the old, characteristic *cuevas* on the Albaicín, a district that besides being Arabian is decidedly Gypsy.

The characteristic bazaar of the Alcaicería, rebuilt in Moorish style at the end of the last century.

LA ALCAICERIA

Next to the Palacio Arzobispal and in front of the Plaza de Bibarrambla, the Alcaiceria, sprawls an ancient Arab silk bazaar, now invaded by tourism. It is an example of how the Moorish spirit lived on in this Christian nucleus. The same reigning spirit is felt in the Corral del Carbón, and in the nearby streets and is the only example of *fondouk* or Arab inn in Europe.

A WALK AROUND GRANADA

The Moslem Alhambra and Christian Cathedral have not exhausted the monumental wealth of the city. It is necessary to organize some walks to discover other monuments which are only excelled by the omnipresence of the two main structures.

The first walk takes us to the **University**, founded in 1526 and later set up in a XVIII century Jesuit school. Next to the university, we can admire the Renaissance church of S. Justo and Pastor and the Colegio Mayor of S. Bartholomé and Santiago, both dating back to the XVI century. But the most interesting part of this walk are two nearby churches: the Iglesia de S. Jerónimo by Siloé which houses the tomb of Gonzalo de Córdoba, the Great Captain, with two Renaissance and Gothic patios and the Iglesia de S. Juan de Dios, one of the best Baroque architectural archievements in Granada with its façade decorated with bas-reliefs and statues. Next to it, the **Hospital de S. Juan de Dios** features a monumental staircase in one of its courtyards.

The large façade with towers of the Basilica of St. John of God.

The façade of St. Jerome and the multi-coloured, sculptured Renaissance retablo.

The simple,
plain façade of the Carthusian monastery.

The "Coro de legos", inside the Carthusian monastery, with
paintings by Sanchez Cotán.

The splendid high altar with its canopy inside the Carthusian ▶
monastery.

The refectory, with the stories of St. Bruno of Cotán, in one of the ▶
few remaining parts of the old XVIth century monastery.

LA CARTUJA

From St. Cristopher's viewpoint, we can walk to another interesting monument, la Cartuja, now known as the «Baroque Alhambra». Founded by Fernando Gonzalo de Cordoba in 1516, it only consists of the church, the sacristy, and cloister with some annexes. After walking through the silver doorway and past a great staircase we reach a type of hallway where we find the first paintings by Sanchez Cotán who, as already mentioned, was a Carthusian monk; we then visit the extravagantly decorated choir and choir stalls. The presbytery, dominated by an Assumption under a canopy, lies opposite it. The nave is surrounded by a series of Bocanegra paintings including the «Conception» at first thought to be painted by Alonso Cano, and another four paintings

by Sanchez Cotán filled with an aura of mystic symplicity which was characteristic of this monk-artist. From behind the altar we enter the **Holy Sanctuary**, a small lavish Baroque room built by Francisco Hurtado Izquierdo in the first quarter of the XVIII century.

The tabernacle is formed by a canopy resting on columns covering the pavillon and is used as a sanctuary. The sculptures are by José Risueño and Duque Cornejo. The same frenetic style of the columns prevails in this section. We can feel this movement in the frescoes by Palomino and Reina in the copper dome like the angels wings and saints vestments stirred by the breath of the Holy Spirit.

The church and sanctuary's lavish decorations are ex-

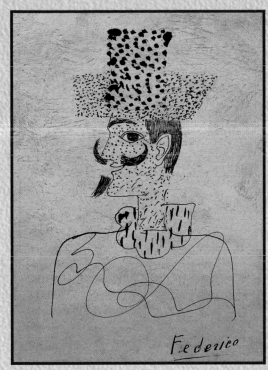

Salvador Dalí, *Self-portrait dedicated to Lorca*, ink on paper, 22 x 16 cm, Mollet (Barcelona), Juan Abello Prat collection.

Federico García Lorca

Federico García Lorca, son of a landowner and destined to become not only a sensitive, creative poet, but also an expert on Andalusian spirit, was born in Fuentevaqueros (Granada) in 1898. His knowledge of Andalusian temperament was no doubt due to his infancy in the countryside of this region, his studies at Almería and in the faculty of Letters and Law at Granada University. Yet, Castile was the place that influenced his first work, *Impressions and Landscapes* (1918). Moreover, Madrid attracted him towards music, the theatre and art, and gave him the opportunity to meet great artists like Dalí and Buñuel. But it was Andalusian spirit that was behind the work that brought him success and exerted so much influence on modern literature, from *Songs* (1927) to *Mariana Pineda* (still in 1927), from *Gypsy Ballads* (1928) to *Poema del Canto Jondo* (1931), from *Blood Wedding* (1933) to *Yerma* (1934) and *The House of Bernarda Alba* (1936). And he met with his tragic destiny in Andalusia: having gone back to Granada as he always did every Summer, the poet was arrested in July 1936 by the Francoist Civil Guards and, although he had never participated directly in any political activity, he was shot on 19th August of that year.

celled by Arévalo and Cabello's baroque **Sacristy**, to which we gain access through a door on the right. Here the columns, panels, capitals, domes and even the floor are overcome by the same frenzy. The Moresque geometric and linear architecture of the Alhambra is in direct contrast with the disordered and disruptive Baroque style.

As Pemán beatifully writes: «We are standing before a symphony of Lamjarón marble, carved stone, mirrors, cream plaster, silver inlays, ivory, ebony, etc. forming an architectural earthquake».

It is not difficult, on the other hand, to think of the relationship of this vivid scene with the Creole-Christian ornaments in South American churches. In comparison, in the refectory besides the cloister, we come across the stark simplicity of the Gothic domes depicting the simple scenes of St. Bruno's life by Sanchez Cotán. The painting of the Carthusian order's holy founder which for a long time was attributed to Alonso Cano, is in fact by Mora and according to a well-known joke among the guides, if you remain silent it's because you're Carthusian...

The sumptuous, rich decoration of the sacristy, attributed to Luis de Arévalo.

In the Albaicín district the Arab Baths are still standing, with their Roman and Visigothic capitals dating back to the XIth century.

ALBAICIN

Another palace to visit at all costs is the sister hill of the Alhambra, the Albaicín, which was the first Moorish colony set up by the Moors who came from Baeza; the name *Rabad al Baecin* comes from here. After the Christian conquest, the Moors united in this redoubt until the Christmas revolt in 1568 when many were massacred and the majority were expelled.

However the Moresque influence prevails over this area. Walking along the steep streets, we come across small squares, patios filled with flowers, Moorish houses and important churches and monuments. The *Iglesia de San Nicolas* is worth visiting as you can enjoy a splendid view of the Alhambra. So is the *Iglesia de San Sal-*

vador, a Mudejar church erected on the site of an ancient mosque. From the *Iglesia de San Cristóbal* we can enjoy an interesting view over the Alcazaba Cadima and its enclosure, built in the XI century on the remains of a Visigothic wall.

The Bañuelo, **Arab baths**, attract many tourists; although they are in a bad state of repair, they are still worth visiting just to see their Visigothic and Roman columns, beside the Moresque ones. «The baths seemingly date back to the XI century and are the most important example of Arab public baths in Spain and the oldest works in Moslem Granada», states Gallego Burín.

The flamenco

One of the most spectacular, passionate elements of the colourful and fiery Andalusian nature is undoubtedly the flamenco, that rhythmic, noble dance that personifies life, with its overwhelming joys and its intense anguish. Typical of Andalusia and with a gypsy background, the flamenco as we know it today began to take shape and become more explicit only in the XVIII century, with a skilful blend of miscellaneous influences, from Moorish to Jewish, and a touch of oriental flavour. The rhythm itself, which is produced by hand-clapping, by the percussive sound of guitar chords and very often by castanets, is extremely fast, but still cannot be considered definitely classified: the dancers (the *bailaora* – the female dancer and the real leader in the performance, with her typical, brightly coloured costume that swirls out like a fan – and the *bailaor*) end up by improvising the choreography of their dance. They also glean inspiration from the warm, throaty voice of the solo singer, the *cantaor*, who accompanies the dance by singing the traditional airs now known as *cante jondo* – 'deep ballads'. In spite of the flamenco being typical of Andalusia, and although it is impregnated with deep, nostalgic melancholy while the movements are charged with vitality, it has become very popular not only in all the other Spanish regions but even farther afield, distinguishing itself throughout the world as an enthralling, captivating performance.

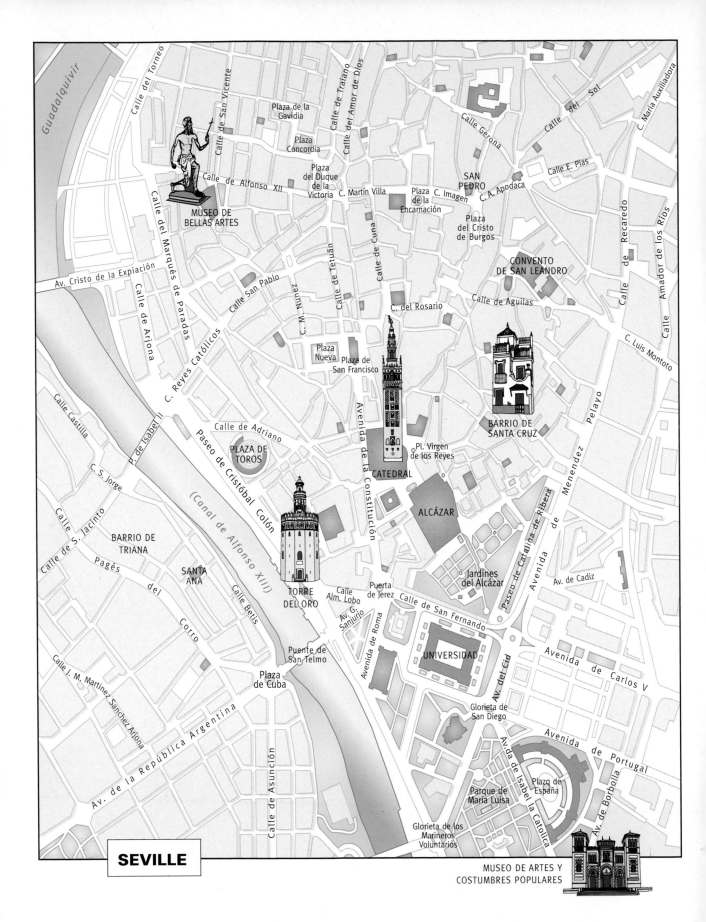

SEVILLE

Guadalquivir

Calle del Torneo
Calle de San Vicente
Calle de Trajano
Calle del Amor de Dios
Plaza de la Gavidia
Plaza Concordia
Calle Gerona
Calle del Sol
C. Maria Auxiliadora
Calle de Alfonso XII
Plaza del Duque de la Victoria
SAN PEDRO
Calle E. Pias
MUSEO DE BELLAS ARTES
C. Martín Villa
Plaza de la Encarnación
C. Imagen
C. C. A. Apodaca
Calle de Recaredo
Calle de Amador de los Ríos
Calle de
Av. Cristo de la Expiación
Calle del Marqués de Paradas
Calle de Ariona
Calle San Pablo
Calle de Tetuán
C. M. Núñez
Calle de Cuna
C. del Rosario
Plaza del Cristo de Burgos
Calle de Aguilas
CONVENTO DE SAN LEANDRO
C. Luis Montoto
C. Reyes Católicos
Plaza Nueva
Plaza de San Francisco
BARRIO DE SANTA CRUZ
Pelayo
Calle Castilla
Calle de Adriano
PLAZA DE TOROS
Avenida de la Constitución
CATEDRAL
Pl. Virgen de los Reyes
Paseo de Catalina de Ribera
Avenida de Menendez
P. de Isabel II
Paseo de Cristóbal Colón
(Canal de Alfonso XIII)
C. S. Jorge
TORRE DEL ORO
ALCÁZAR
Avenida de
Av. de Cadiz
Calle de S. Jacinto
BARRIO DE TRIANA
Pagés
SANTA ANA
Calle Betis
Calle Alm. Lobo
Puerta de Jerez
Jardines del Alcázar
del Corro
Av. G. Sanjurio
Calle de San Fernando
Av. del Cid
Avenida de Carlos V
Puente de San Telmo
Avenida de Roma
UNIVERSIDAD
Calle J. M. Martínez Sánchez Arjona
Plaza de Cuba
Glorieta de San Diego
Avenida de Portugal
Av. de la República Argentina
Calle de Asunción
Av.da de Isabel la Católica
Plaza de España
Av. de Borbolla
Parque de María Luisa
Glorieta de los Marineros Voluntarios
MUSEO DE ARTES Y COSTUMBRES POPULARES

*Once the site of capital punishments,
the Plaza de la Falange Española
is today Seville's administrative centre.*

SEVILLE

Seville, the gracious city, the quintessence of Andalusia. When one thinks of Seville, one immediately has visions of crying Virgins and suffering Christs being carried through the streets during Easter, or knights with beatiful maidens riding through the city during the April festivities. Like the greatest cities, it rose from a myth that «Hercules built it». Phoenicians, Greeks, Carthaginians and Romans conquered it or were conquered by it. The old Hispalis is the best paradigm of Andalusian history. When it was the capital of the Visigothic reign it was overthrown by the Moors in 712 and in glory it rivaled with the neighbouring Sultan Cordova. Buildings rose up after the Almohad invasion in the XII century.

A century later the Holy King Ferdinand entered the city and died there beside his sword and standard. The Christian Monarchs then set up their court over Mohammedan castles. But the city's most glorious mo-ment was when it became the capital of two new worlds, Lope de Vega's «new Babylon» where the noble and courageous contrasted with the poor: a world of American treasures, great enterprises, religious ideals, theological dogma, art and literal principles alongside a world of beggars and tramps, the true characters of minor history.

Its political decadence was similar to the country's general apathy, which increased due to some domestic tragedies, like the terrible plague in 1649 causing the death of many famous artists. But its past splendour and glory can still be felt in the unique monumental relics and the same vitality and sparkling humanity still reign over Seville which made it not only the capital of this extensive region, which stretches over the Sierra to the sea, but also the official capital of Andalusia as the seat of its autonomous government and centre of social and political problems.

◀ *A suggestive view of the Giralda, symbol of the city.*

A general view over the massive structure of the Cathedral, the third largest church in the Christian world.

THE CATHEDRAL AND ITS BELL-TOWER

The Christians built their own temple on the site of the main Mosque. However they kept the mosque's minaret which they used as the bell-tower and the Patio de los Naranjos as an unusual cloister. A great part of Seville's spirit characterizes this inseparable symbiosis.

The **Giralda**, which was in fact a Muslim minaret but cleverly disguised by the Marian symbolism of faith depicted with its four terraces with lilies, is an outstanding symbol of Seville and is one of the most beautiful and admired towers in the world.

The minaret was erected during the Almohad period near the end of the XII century; there are two sister towers also built by the Almohades: the Hassan, in Rabat, and the Kutnbis in Marrakech. The tower, almost 100 metres high, is decorated outside with arabesques

and mullioned windows which give it a delicate touch. The work was put in the hands of the poet Arubequer Benzoar by the Emir Abu Yusuf Al Mansur. Inside the tower is a solid ramp which the Christian conqueror King Ferdinand the Saint rode over a few years later. The tower was completed with four gold-plated bronze globes but an earthquake destroyed them and they were replaced in 1568 with four Renaissance elements supporting the popular weather-cock (in fact it is a revolving weather-cock and certainly isn't an appropriate symbol of faith but in Seville...) which gave its name to the whole tower.

The Gothic style dominates the cathedral which was commenced in 1420, although later work was Renaissance. According to legend, the town council appointed

*From the top of the Giralda,
one can fully appreciate the cross-shaped
structure of the Cathedral.*

all the famous architects, sculptors and stone-masons to build the greatest temple on earth, and they almost succeded as Seville cathedral is depicted on the floor of the Vatican in Rome, as the third biggest Christian temple, only excelled by St. Peter's itself, Saint Paul's in London and by the new Abidjan cathedral. It is 130 metres long, 76 metres wide and features 68 domes supported by 40 solid pillars as well as 93 stained-glass windows which let light filter through and shine on thousands of shadowy figures and statues made of marble, clay, iron, wood, and stone and on a whole cosmic world of friezes, capitals, altarpieces, tombs and stained-glass windows.

The work on the building continued from 1502 to 1519. In 1511 the dome was destroyed and later rebuilt by Gil de Hontanón. The most famous architects who contributed were Juan Norman, Pedro de Toledo, Juan de Alava, Gil de Hontánon, (Dome) Diego de Riaño and Martin de Gainza (Sacristy of the Chalices) Juan de Meda (Royal Chapel). Some of the greatest artists expressed their talent here: Pedro de Campaña, Roelas, Herrera el Mozo, Murillo, Zurbarán, Valdés, Alejo Fernandez, Alonso Cano and Luis de Vergas. Sculptors like

Fancelli, Andrea della Robbia, Martinez Montañés, Miguel Perrin, etc. performed the terracotta decoration and marble tombs; Nufro Sanchez built the choir and Dancart achieved the choir-stalls; Arfe engraved the monstrance in silver creating «the best and oldest existing work of art in silver while Bartolomeo Morel worked in bronze; Francisco de Salamanca, Antonio de Palencia, Sancho Munoz, Juan de Yepes, Esteban and Diego Idoboro worked with wrought iron.

When you enter this immense church you enter into a world of art where every piece is worth looking at, but there are a few special items which deserve a closer look.

First of all there is the **Capilla Mayor** which houses the oldest Christian *altarpiece*, lost in a symphony of shapes and colour. It is 200 square metres in size with more than a thousand figures depicting the holy story. No less than 26 artists from different parts of the world worked on this piece, the first being a Fleming, Dancart, in 1482, followed by Bernardo and Francisco Ortega, Jorge Fernandez, etc. The central part was finished in 1521, while the work on the sides was carried out from 1550 to 1564 by Diego Vazquel, Nurfo

*A detail of the Nativity
in the Cathedral's retablo.*

The external part of the Royal Chapel's
apse erected in plateresque style.

The altar of the Royal Chapel, with the ▶
venerated statue of the Virgen de los Reyes.

de Ortega, Juan López, Pedro de Heredia, etc. It consists of 45 paintings of the life of Christ and the Virgin Mary together with paintings of the principal Sevillian saints. This huge, illuminating cosmos of paintings, figurines and canopies are used as the background for all great ceremonies or for the graceful dance of the «six» during the public holiday of the Immaculate Conception or Corpus Christi. The dance of the «six» is a traditional Sevillian dance where the choir boys appointed to sing at religious ceremonies dress up as page-boys from the XVI century and have the privilege of dancing in front of the Arfe monstrance. They are simple ancient Spanish dances, like the Bolero, whose gracefulness and lightness contrast strikingly with the elaborate velvet and gold reflections inside the cathedral.

In the Museum of Arts and Popular Traditions you can follow the evolution of the costumes and traditions of the Sevillian «six».

The magnificent railings which enclose the main chapel and which seem to reflect the multi-coloured altarpiece with its «Plateresque style», are by Francisco de Salamanca and Sancho Muñoz who together carried out the work from 1518 to 1533.

Behind the main chapel stands the Renaissance **Capilla Real**, built at the beginning of 1551 by Martin de Gainza who was succeded by Hernan Ruiz; it was then completed by Juan de Maeda in 1575. The chapel conceived as a Royal Pantheon houses the tombs of two of Sevillian's most famous figures. The first is *Alfonso X the Wise*, who, encouraged by his mother Beatrix of Swabia, proceeded to reign unsuccessfully in the Sevillian castles; a dream which came true many years later

The Sacristía de los Cálices,
in flamboyant Gothic style, features
on its altar a beautiful Crucifix sculptured
in 1603 by Montáñes.

The plateresque Sacristía Mayor houses the large
Renaissance ostensory in silver by
Juan de Arfe, weighing 300 kilograms.

In the head of the Cathedral's transept, ▶
four figures representing the Spanish kings
support the sarcophagus with the presumed
mortal remains of Christopher Columbus.

for Charles V; the tomb of his mother lies opposite.

In the centre, in front of the high altar, stands a rich XVIII century silver arch, a gift from Philip V which guards the tomb of another great Sevillian figure, the Holy King Ferdinand III; he conquered the Saracen power and is the city's patron saint: «the loyalest, truest, noblest, most honest and humble king» according to the epigraph written in Latin, Muslem, Hebrew and Spanish.

The two XVI century sacristies, the **Sacristia Mayor** and **Sacristia de los Calices** are both authentic museums within the cathedral. Amidst the opulent setting of the Sacristia Mayor we can admire the Silver Montrance by Juan de Arfe and the so-called «tablas alfonsinas», a *triptych shrine* and gift from Alfonso X. The treasure honours its name with numerous chalices, shrines and religious offerings. Mention must be made of *Goya's paintings*, depicting the Sevillian saints, Justa and

Rufina, the popular «cacharreras». Paintings by Murillo, Morales (*Pietà*), Valdes Leal, Tritan etc. A moving *crucifix* by Martinez Montañés presides over this small art gallery which one comes across before leaving the cathedral. Our curiosity will be aroused by a pompous collection of sculptures which are one of the latest additions to the temple's treasures. We are referring to the romantic tomb of **Christopher Columbus**, by Arturo Melida. It was brought here in 1899 from the Habana cathedral and is only a symbolic tomb as it is empty.

A typical statue of Christopher stands behind it, a statue easily found in other cathedrals as according to tradition, whoever looks at Saint Christopher is guaranteed the following 24 hours of life. If we look up at the domes we can see some XIX century stained-glass windows together with more valuable ones executed in the XVI century by Flemish artists.

Holy Week

Religion and folklore blend together in Andalusia for Holy Week, seven days of solemn celebrations throughout the whole of Spain, with throngs participating in processions and following parades with enormous floats practically everywhere. Nevertheless, Andalusia is the place where participation is most devote and enthusiastic during the week be-

tween Palm Sunday and Easter Day. In Seville, for example, about a hundred huge, golden floats called *pasos*, loaded with crucifixes and votive images that sometimes recreate episodes of the Passion, are taken up and down the streets many times. On Holy Wednesday, a tremendous detonation like a clap of thunder is fired to shatter the silence in the Cathedral, recalling the time when the veil in the Jerusalem Temple was ripped. Another identical 'clap of thunder' is produced during Midnight Mass on the night between Holy Saturday and Easter Sunday, and is the signal for all bells to start ring-

ing. The huge crowds always participate actively in these celebrations, reciting prayers and singing hymns, some of which are very old and known as *saetas*. At the same time, repentant sinners covered from head to toe in long tunics and pointed hoods, walk the streets non-stop and plead forgiveness for their sins.

*Two images of the Patio de los Naranjos, which
is the court-yard of the old almohade mosque.
Planted with orange trees and decorated
with a fountain, it is a fascinating, enchanted
place dominated by the Gothic façade of the Cathedral.*

PATIO DE LOS NARANJOS

The **Patio de los Naranjos** is the only cloister in the cathedral. It was once the patio of an ancient mosque and is mentioned in all the best-loved clichés about the city. The scent of the orange-blossom in the spring air seems to mingle with the murmuring of the beggars and the cripples who used to sit on the steps outside and even today we still find them waiting for tourists.

There is a fountain in the middle which comes from a Visigothic cathedral. A curious object is found beside the Lagarto door, through an original Mosque arch; it is a wooden crocodile hanging from the roof which gave rise to well-known legends of princesses and dragons; however, it is seemingly a saurian replica which was sent to Alfonso X by the Sultan of Egypt in 1260, at a time when such a reptile was considered a monster in these parts.

From the Giralda, a view over the Alcazar's battlemented walls and towers.

LOS REALES ALCAZARES

Despite the Arab influence which reigns in these palaces, little in fact remains of the first Moresque constructions. Only the wall around the castle is still standing, containing the **Puerta del León** on the entrance to the Alcazar dating back to the XII century. The enclosure continues right up to the river with the Torre de Abdelaziz, the Torre de la Plata, and the **Torre del Oro** which faced another sister tower on the other side of the riverbed, hence forming a barrier to prevent enemy ships from entering. The **Patio del Yeso** also forms part of the early structure and is a unique example of Almohad architecture in Spain.

But fires, earthquakes, reforms and later extensions either wiped out or absorbed these early structures. What we see now is the castle of King Peter, one of the most complete examples of Mudejar art, that is to say, a Christian palace finished by Islamic or Christian craftsmen with a Muslem artistic training. The castle of King Peter I of Castile, nick-named the Cruel King, was completed in the XIV century; later, extensions and alterations were made and unfortunately badly-planned Romantic restorations were carried out. The Catholic Monarchs appointed Moorish craftsmen to work on it. Then, in 1526, to celebrate Charles V wedding, it underwent some extensions and further modernizations were carried out under Philip V in 1624. All in all, it is still one of the best examples of Mudejar art, this unusual Spanish style which was formed on Christian soil from an Islamic and Jewish tradition during a transitional era when Christian intolerance hadn't yet ruined the co-existence of Christian, Islamic and Jewish cultures.

The Mudejar art here is over-loaded with colour and imagination and lies on the border-line of the sublime and Kitsch, typical of the oldest cliché of Andalusian «bad taste» and Spanish traditionalism. José Péman amusingly points out that «King Peter» was an Andalusian type «orientalist» which anticipated the orientalism of Zorilla or of Villaespesa, imitating the style of Baghdad.

It wouldn't be right to generalize too much on Andalusian constructions by calling the Palace or the Alhambra Arabic or by ignoring the strong Roman influence in Cordova, like the Roman columns found in the Mosque.

The Puerta del Léon, which opens in the circuit of walls, is crowned by an azulejo with a rampant lion.

The Patio de la Montería, whose name originates from that of the royal guard, the Monteros de Espinosa.

After walking through the Puerta del Léon, we find the Patio de la Monteria which dates back to the times of Mexuar and which separates the palace from the city; we then reach the Patio del Leon where we can admire the main façade of the palace, erected in 1364 and whose wings were later enlarged in the XVI and XVII centuries. On the second part of this façade a Cufic inscription praising Allah is engraved next to the Gothic inscription in memory of the creator of the work.

The **Patio de las Doncellas**, surrounded by lobe-shaped arches, forms the central nucleus of the residence. On the walls there are delicately engraved plasterwork and XVI enamel tile panels which are the best examples of Mudejar art.

The Patio de las Doncellas is characterized by
a rich decoration of azulejos, dating back
to the XVIth century and undoubtedly the most beautiful
in the entire palace, and by multi-coloured
lacunar ceilings.

An example of the splendid mudéjar decoration ▶
that covers walls as well as door frames and
arches in the Salón de Embajadores.

The soft and delicate finishing touch is accentuated by the colourful panelling and doors. Following Arabic tradition, all public and ceremonial activities took place here, while the private life evolved around the Patio de las Muñecas; the names of the rooms are arbitary and originate from traditional everyday life.

The rooms which surround the Patio de las Doncellas are more official in character. They consist of the Charles V «Salón del techo», named after the lavish Renaissance cedar-wood lacunar ceiling; three small rooms of Maria de Padilla and the main room, which is also the most beatiful in the castle, the **Salón de Embajadores**. In the front archway, the repetitive Nazarene inscription «Only God is victorious» is engraved in Arabic. The doors were carved by Toledan craftsmen. Apart from the dome, the rest of the decoration is of the King Peter period; it was carried out in the XV century and later restored. There is a surprising series of portraits of all the Spanish kings up to Philip III with their coats-of-arms and dates of their reigns, set in Gothic arches. The room at the end is the dining-room with Philip II period panelling.

The **Patio de las Muñecas**, the centre of the private quarters, is elegant. The columns date back to the Caliph period and come from the then-devastated Cordovan Medina Zahara (the stuccoes of the upper part were re-made in 1843).

After climbing up a Charles V period staircase with

The high dome of the Salón de Embajadores
built in 1420 with its complicated arabesques
and covered in gilded stalactites.

The Salón de Embajadores, whose mudéjar style ▶
decoration dates back to the times of Peter I,
is one of the most beautiful rooms in the Alcazar.

beautiful XVI century enamel tiles, we reach a series of rooms decorated with Flemish, French and Spanish XVII and XVIII century tapestries. In the **Oratorio de los Reyes Católicos** there are more tiles which form a small altar, painted by Niculoso Pisano in 1504. Next we come to the Salas de los Infantes de Reyes, King Peter's bedroom and that of Doña Maria with more panelling and enamel tiles.

From the Patio del León we reach the **Salas de los almirantes** which houses the Casa de la Contratación; it is where some of the most important voyages to the new world, like Magellan's trip round the world, were planned. The walls are covered with XVII and XVIII tapestries, and in the famous painting «*la Virgen de los navagantes*» by Alejo Fernandez, many people claim to have seen the effigy of Colombus on the right, surrounded by the Pinzón brothers.

From the Patio del León we also reach the Patio de Maria de Padilla, which stands among a series of structures built during the XVIII century, during Philip V's reign, over the ruins of a Gothic palace dating back to either the end of the XIII or the beginning of the XIV century with only a few half-buried traces left, like the arcade known as the Baños de Maria de Padilla. The Gothic chapel, a wide room which was made into an oratory by Philip V, and a Charles V room are to be found among these Gothic buildings.

In the chapel, there are XVI century enamel tiles and a XVIII century Baroque altarpiece. The splendid *Nativity* from the Granada School stands out in the collec-

tion of paintings. In Charles V's room, with a roof made of ogival domes and tiles painted by Cristobál de Augusta in 1577, there is a splendid tapestry collection in bright colours depicting the adventures of the emperor during the conquest of Tunis. They were made by Pannemaker in 1554 from the canvases of Jan Cornelius Vermeyen, the artist who accompanied the emperor during the war expedition in 1535 (some of them are not originals as they were replaced by imitations in the XVIII century).

Other Flemish XVII century tapestries are exhibited in the Salón del Emperador depicting the Creation of Man. In this room we also find some good examples of XVI century Andalusian enamel tiles.

The Arab-Andalusian tradition of having an important and complementary place inside the court residences gave rise to the **Jardínes del Alcazar**. They were later changed by successive residents.

Charles V added a *Pavilion* with galleries of columns and beautiful enamel tiles by Juan Hernández (1543), dominating the section named after the king. Avenues lined with palm-trees and geometric box-wood

The Patio de las Muñecas or Patio of the Dolls is thus named owing to the female heads on the capitals.

◄ *In the Cuarto del Almirante, the retablo of the Madonna of the sailors is kept; the figure to the right at the Virgin's feet is a portrait of Columbus.*

The Gardens of the Alcazar, laid out in terraces and planted with orange trees and palms, are examples of the finest Andalusian art.

paths which widen out to protect a spring on ground level or a fountain here and there form a picture of classic Renaissance peacefulness. Then the neo-classic *Los Grutescos* were placed there. The large pond, which reflects the tops of the palm-trees, features a *bronze fountain* of Mercury by Diego Pesquera. The pied-à-terre, a large room with marble columns, leads onto the Patio de Banderas; from there we can reach the Plaza del Triunfo, outside the enclosure, whose name brings to mind images of horse-driven carriages parked at this point. There are all types of gardens from the Arab period right up to the present day. But, however different they may be, they are all characterized by the same Andalusian spirit filled with the sweet, light perfume of the orange and lemon blossoms and jazmine flowers, and the soft trickling of the water from the springs and fountains which reflects the colourful glazes of the tiles.

SEVILLE, THE NEW BABYLON

Spain's Golden Age, with the political unification of the country and discovery of the new land filling it with the soldiers, missionaries, saints, theologians and beggars was also the golden age for Seville. Lope de Vega who dedicated some of his talents to her, called the city the «New Babylon». The fact that the Guadalquivir was still navigable and the city had a port explains its sudden boom.

As a result of this change, Seville was overcome with many types of palaces, convents, churches, monuments and houses which are still standing today. To complete this picture of the city, it is worth mentioning some of the best known structures.

CASA LONJA

The **Plaza del Triunfo** lies between the cathedral and the castle's walls and houses a pretentious monument in memory of the Sevillian theologians who explained the *Immaculate Conception* of the Virgin Mary hence earning the official Marian title: the **Casa Lonja** which rises up admist the palm-trees, and houses the **Archive of India**, built by Herrera between 1583 and 1598 to be used as the Exchange or Casa de Contratación to deal with business with the West Indies. But the Archive remained there when it was set up in 1784. All the documents regarding the discovery of America, conquests, and later discoveries are kept here for reference for experts and researchers.

HOSPITAL DE LA CARIDAD

The Hospital de la Caridad was founded in the XVI century as the seat of an Association whose pious tasks were to comfort prisoners sentenced to death just before they were executed and to give the executed a Christian burial. Its founder was Don Miguel de Manara, a cocky young Sevillian gentleman who finally repented and converted to charity to redeem his past. His character also inspired the famous universal mythical figure of Don Juan Tenorio referred to by writers and musicians like Tirso de Molina, Zorrilla, Molière, Mozart, Max Frisch, Maranon, etc.

THE TOWN HALL

The Town hall stands on the opposite side of the Cathedral, dominating both the Plaza Nueva and de San Francisco where the famous and most lively Calle Sierpes begins, filled with classical Cervantine rendez-vous. It was built in 1527 according to designs by Diego de Riano and is a fundamental example of «Plateresque» art, Renaissance art with rich decorations formed by the delicate gold and silver work of its craftsmen. Besides its interesting architecture, it also contains some first class paintings and artistic objects.

The statue of the Immaculate Conception on the Plaza del Triunfo.

The severe façade of the Casa Lonja, which houses the Archives of the Indies, invaluable due to the History of the Spanish colonisation of America.

The charming façade with azulejos of the Hospital de la Caridad.

The back façade of the Ayuntamiento opens onto the Plaza Nueva.

The patio of the Casa de Pilatos, with the double row of 24 arches and a very fine embossed decoration of azulejos.

CASA DE PILATOS

The Casa de Pilatos owned by the Dukes of Medinaceli, is one of the most luxurious mansions in Seville, due to its architectural wealth and art collections. Built at the end of the XV century, it combines the Mudejar, Renaissance and Gothic styles. According to legend, it is thus named as it is a true reproduction of the palace of Pontius Pilate in Jerusalem. Rooms, which have been converted into an interesting museum of classic statuary, open up onto the main patio, with the best example of Spanish enamel tiles.

The eighteenth century
Puerta de la Macarena, near to the
homonymous basilica.

The venerated statue of the Virgen ▶
de la Macarena, attributed
to the sculptress Luisa Roldán.

THE GRACIOUS CITY

There is no other city in Spain, or in the world according to some Sevillians, as gracious as Seville; the omnipresence of happiness, openness, good humour, imagination and love of life which dominates every gesture, saying and corner of the city, make it unique.

We obviously can't «visit» their gestures and sayings but we can feel them immediately as soon as we enter the city. The true graceful character is reflected in the street corners which are crammed together forming their own districts and well worth visiting.

The most famous quarter in the world is undoubtedly the *Barrio de Santa Cruz*, a small maze hidden between the castle walls and the Murillo gardens. A fantastic world with its evocative street names like Callejón del

Agua, Calle de la Pimienta, Vida, Jamerdana, Mezquita, Cruces etc. In the *Plaza de Santa Cruz* there is a XVIII century wrought iron cross and it reminds us of the folklore tradition of the «cruces de mayo» or May crosses. In every street there are balconies adorned with flowers, garden walls covered with jazmines and doorways filled with flowers and fountains. It isn't a typical ancient Moorish quarter as one might think; in fact the «barrio» was «invented» in the XX century by the most famous Spanish expert on tourism, the Marquis de la Vega Inclán, who also invented the Toledan Casa del Greco and other things of the same style.

Another world famous district is the **Triana barrio**. Rodrigo de Triana was the first man to catch sight of

The Barrio de Santa Cruz,
with its whitewashed houses.

The Cruz de Cerranjería dating back
to 1695, with its elaborate
wrought-iron volutes.

The Hospital de Venerables Sacerdotes houses ▶
the Museo de la Semana Santa, with
its numerous "pasos", groups portraying passion
which, mounted on floats, are paraded along
the streets during the Holy Week.

the New Land, and later many things and people were named after him, for example the river bank of Seville when the river was still navigable as well as bull fighters, dancers, etc. Although nowadays it has lost its original physical and urbanistic form, it hasn't lost its spiritual identity. The Trianeros are proud of belonging to Triano and when they carry their Virgin, Esperanza de Triana, they fight, if necessary, with the people from the enemy district who are devoted to the «Macarena», the rival Virgin who characterizes and animates the whole area with its pure Sevillian Basilica, which stands in front of a triumphal doorway, and is overcome by mystery and movement at midnight on Holy Thursday.

◄ *A view of the Park of Maria Luisa, with its lush vegetation and romantic corners. Below, a view of the Plaza de España.*

Plaza de España, surrounded by the impressive buildings of the Iberian-American show held in 1929.

PARQUE DE MARIA LUISA

The parks and gardens scattered around the city form the framework of this picture. There are ancestral gardens, like the castle's gardens, municipal ones like the Murillo garden, or noble gardens like the famous Parque de Maria Luisa. A romantic park used as a setting for sweet Spanish melodies and whose avenues are named after the Swans or the most important Romantic poet of Spain, the Sevillian Gustavo Adolfo Bécquer. Summerhouses, pathways, horse-driven carriages, pools filled with water lilies and labyrinths of enamel tiles all form a perfectly romantic setting.

Pavilions for the great Hispo-American Fair were set up here in 1929. And what could have in fact been the park's downfall, turned out to be its crowning glory. Permanent structures were built for the occasion, like the **Plaza de España** which was created with traditional materials (fashionable tiles, enamel tiles, imagination, colour) and which now plays an important role in the scenario of Seville.

The destiny of the Parque de Maria Luisa is definitely linked to the theme of America. Apart from holding the Hispo-American Exhibition there and naming its streets and avenues after heroes of the Latin-American era, its other great square is in fact called the **Plaza de America**. An oval area surrounded by gardens, terraces and doves, now strongly connected to Andalusia. In fact one of the three pavilions which stands at one of the ends, the **Pabellón Real**, is now the seat of the Council or Autonomous Government of Andalusia. The other two pavilions opposite are more interesting for tourists: the Pabellón Renacimiento, on the south side, houses the **Archaeological Museum of Seville**, one of the most interesting museums in the country for its statuary and Roman antiques as Andalusia was one of the most romanized provinces of the Empire. There are also pre-Roman exhibits, like the Carambolo Treasure which dates back to the native civilisation of the «Turdetanos».

The façade of the Archaelogical Museum, rich in works of art.

In the Plaza de América stands the pavilion that houses the interesting Museo de Artes y Costumbres Populares.

Above the Paseo de Cristóbal Colón rises the Golden Tower, thus named because it was once covered in gilded azulejos.

The bridge called La Barqueta. ▶

   The north pavilion is called the «Pabellón Mudéjar» and houses the **Museum of Art and Popular Customs**. A visit is necessary to find out about traditional ways of life in Seville. There is a vast collection of pieces of furniture, household objects, ceramics, clothes, jewels games, bullfighting articles, etc.
   On the subject of bullfighting, mention must be made of the most beautiful and well-known bull ring in the world, the **Real Plaza de la Maestranza**. It was built in 1760, and touched up later, with lavish stone and tiles resting on marble columns, where the most famous bull fighters such as Joselito and Belmonte risked death.

The Expo

The year 1992 was a very important one for Spain since it became the centre of international interest due to a series of events occurring simultaneously: that was the five hundredth anniversary of the discovery of America, an event that changed world history and in which the great Iberian Peninsula had played a fundamental role. Hence, Barcelona was selected to hold the 1992 *Olympic Games*, in spectacular and futuristic scenery, whereas Seville was chosen as the site for the *Expo '92*, an extremely important world-wide event, which partially changed the appearance of this peaceful Andalusian city. The most appropriate site for the Universal Exhibition, where all the most recent technological and scientific discoveries would be presented, was identified in the *Isla de la Cartuja*, on the banks of the River Guadalquivir. This was where parks were created with educational and cultural themes and where futuristic structures and innovative pavilions, worthy of such an event that looked to the future, were built to house the over 100 participating nations. A monorail railway with an ultra modern train took visitors from one section to another, from the metallic *Castile and León Pavilion* to the unmistakable steeply leaning, blue tower which held the *Andalusia Pavilion*. Not even the XIV century *Santa María de las Cuevas* charterhouse, famous for having accommodated Christopher Columbus among others, 'escaped' from all this; on the contrary, once it had been appropriately restructured it was called upon to participate directly in the event. And when it was all over, these ambitious, striking monuments to the optimism of Mankind in the future, nearly all remained and continue to dominate this enormous part of the city which, due to the exciting and educational experience it had gone through, had definitely changed. Like the *Navigator's Pavilion,* for example, an authentic naval museum on the river embankment, or the *Lago de España* that is now the focal point of a large fairground opened in 1997 and renamed *Isla Mágica*. The exploits of the navigators and explorers of the New World who started their journeys from Seville during the XVI century are all re-enacted here with spectacular pride.

RUINAS DE ITALICA

Another interesting archaeological spot outside Seville, is the Ruinas de Italica. They are the remains of a Roman city which over the centuries was used as a quarry to build mosques, palaces, convents; in the XVI century, the poet Rodrigo Caro described them as being «fields of solitude and despair».

However, you can trace the line of the roads and pavements, the form of the villas with their mosaic floors, the drainage system and urbanisation structures, and the remains of the amphitheatre which gives us an idea of the importance of the city. Next to it stands the **Monasterio de S. Isidoro** which was built with the same stone by Guzmán el Bueno, one of the national heroes who threw down his dagger used to sacrifice his son from the battlements of the fortress rather than handing it over to the Unfaithful in exchange. His body rests there in the shadow of a beautiful altarpiece by Martinez Montañés.

A few kilometres from Seville, one comes across the Roman ruins of Itálica, the town founded by the Scipiones and the birthplace of the Emperor Trajan, Hadrian and Theodosius.

CORDOVA

Cordova is one of the few cities left in the world still characterized by a tremendous feeling of spirit.

Founded by the Carthaginians, conquered by the Romans and invaded by the Goths, it still has preserved, despite the passing of time, the spiritual characteristics of these races. Although only a few Roman remains still stand, the mythical names of Seneca and Lucan live on.

The city's greatest moment came later. After the invasion of the Moors in 711, it became the capital of a vast emirate which continued to grow with the help of a succession of emirs who invaded North Europe, although they were finally defeated in Poitiers. About the middle of the VIII century, an Omeyan prince, immediately after the dynastic change of the Omeyans of Damasco, fled to Cordova and proclaimed himself Emir of Andalusia under the name of Abderraman I. This was the beginning of a glorious age for Cordova, finally reaching its peak with Abderraman III, who proclaimed himself Caliph in 929, with his son Alhaquén II and with the fierce warrior Almanzor, the right-hand man of Caliph Hixam II.

*Cordova seen
from the Cathedral tower.*

During the X century, the «iron age» for the rest of Central and Northern Europe, Cordova continued to boom and became the most densely populated and civilized city in the west, only comparable to the prosperous city of Constantinople. Its mosque became the richest and most splendid Islamic monument. Later another 300 mosques, luxurious palaces, baths, sewer systems and street lighting systems were to follow...

This material wealth was accompanied by intellectual wealth. People like Maimonides, a Jewish doctor and philosopher, Averroes, who introduced Aristotle's philosophy to Europe and the poet Ibn Hazam are key figures in the West's cultural history.

Cordova also filled the gap between Ancient Greek and Roman culture and the rest of Europe.

The abolition of the Omeyan caliph in 1031 followed the breaking-up of Al-Andalus into different rival emirates and its gradual decline. At the beginning of the XIII century, after the final defeat of the Almohades at the Navas de Tolosa, Cordova was taken by Fernando III, the Holy King, and was exposed for many centuries until the Christian unification by the Catholic Monarchs. There were still some glorious moments and the city gave birth to famous people like the Great Captain and the poet Luis de Gongora. The city began to recover from its prostration, felt especially in the XIX century with the 1927 generation; even today it is improving its social and economical problems.

The Patio of Oranges, decorated with palm and orange trees, featuring five fountains.

The exterior of the Mezquita Cathedral, the largest mosque in the Islamic world after Mecca.

The high tower of the Almirar crowned by the statue of the Archangel Raphael.

THE MOSQUE-CATHEDRAL

The main mosque of the Caliphal city was built in 788 by the first caliph, Abderraman I, over the foundation of an old Visigothic temple, which previously stood over the remains of a Roman temple. The pre-existing architectural elements were used to build the mosque and Roman and Visigothic columns and capitals can be seen in the oldest part. Abderraman's son, Hixam I, finished the mosque and added a minaret; in all, the primitive structure consisted of eleven naves perpendicular to the Patio de los Naranjos. Abderraman II enlarged the mosque by extending the naves right up to the river between 833 and 848. Alhaquém II made a further extension by deepening the naves as far as possible, stopped only by the nearness of the river. The *mihrab* built in the *qibla* can still be seen today. Finally, as Almanzor couldn't deepen it, he widened the oratory on one side, adding another eight naves, which made the mihrab off centre. It is easy to identify this part by

From the tower one can observe how solid the walls of the Mezquita are.

One usually gains access to the cathedral through the three arches in Arab style of the Door of Pardon.

its floor by the primitive wall around the enclosure and by the striking uniformity of the capitals and the columns.

During Charles V's reign, the Town Council decided to erect a cathedral amidst the Muslem columns. The work began in 1523, only to be completed two hundred and fifty years later, changing from Gothic to Baroque architecture and from Plateresque to Herrenian style.

Different doors lead to the Patio de los Naranjos; the main door is the *Puerta del Perdón* which is a Mudejar piece. Next to it stands the Herrerian tower only used to strengthen and save the old minaret erected by Abderraman and later used as a model for the Almohad minarets in Rabat and Marrakech. The early minaret is in fact inside the present one.

After crossing the traditional mosque patio, we suddenly find ourselves in an original stone oasis where one retreated to pray. The entwining arches hanging over columns give a palmtree effect which produces a soft and delicate light to accompany the worshipper during his retreat. Going through this oasis of more than eight hundred columns, the most expressive of its kind, we can easily appreciate the other parts of the structure. In the oldest part, there are Visigothic and Roman capitals and columns. The arches above them are made of characteristic red and white bands perhaps inspired by Hispo-Roman structures, like the Merida aqueduct, and which later inspired subsequent Islamic architecture to some extent. After leaving the cathedral and crossing the Villaviciosa chapel and the Royal chapel, we arrive at the *qibla*, the end wall where the *mihrab*, or «sancta sanctorum» stands, facing Mecca; this is where the holy Koran is kept.

The mihrab is logically the most lavish part of the mosque and builders and artists took great care over it. In front of the mihrab, the sublime Caliphal art changes to the elegant Baroque architecture found in the arches hanging above one another, forming a type of entwining architectural mosaic. An example of this Baroque-influenced Arabic art is also found in the Palacio de la Aljafería in Saragossa.

The «qibla» is decorated with a series of lobe-shaped arches, while the floor is covered in golden, ornate mosaics. Underneath lies the *alfiz*, a great slab which acts as a background to the monumental Arab doors. Between the mouldings is an inscription praising Allah and written in gold on a blue background. The Herrarian arch is supported by four columns: two red ones and two green ones which come from the old mihrab of Abderraman II, which once stood where the Villaviciosa chapel now stands. There is a long inscription in memory of the Caliph builder, Albaquen, the creator of this jewel. The panels are finely engraved marble with plant motives.

The interior is covered with an original scallop-shapped dome; marble panels are its leading feature.

The mosaics which cover most of the surface give it its rich and lavish appearance. They are the work of Byzantine artists sent over by the Emperor Niceforo from Constantinople, where mosaic art had reached the height of perfection.

On the right, we come across the *maqsura* which was used exclusively by the Caliph for prayer. Behind it lies a passageway which let the sovereign enter and leave

The mass of columns inside the Mezquita.

The mihrab, characterized by the minute decoration on the walls.

The dome of the mihrab, with its extraordinary ▶ acoustics, was built out of a single block of marble.

the enclosure without mixing with the other worshippers.

The surprising XVI century **Christian cathedral** is to be found amidst the columns; it is certainly of intrisic interest despite its awkward position. The main altar in red marble with paintings by Palomino and the Baroque pulpits help to stimulate this interest. But the most splendid piece is the *chancel*, a master-piece by the Sevillian Pedro Duque Cornejo dating back to the XVII century.

The cathedral's treasure of relics, chalices, an ivory cross attributed to Alonso Cano and the magnificent silver monstrance by Arfe, are kept in the sacristy and in the chapter room.

One of the main tourist attractions is the *Cruz del cautivo*, next to one of the columns alongside the entrance. Supposedly, a captive of the Saracens engraved a Christ on the marble with his nails. According to R. Ramirez de Arellano, in fact, it is only a symbol of possession engraved by the conquerors with their daggers or swords when they had taken over mosques and palaces with their weapons.

There is a string of Christian chapels and additional rooms around the mosque. The *Capilla de San Pablo* is especially interesting with an altarpiece by P. de Céspedes. Although they are trying to restore the mosque to its original splendour, it still remains the most beautiful and most famous mosque of western Muslem art together with the mosque of the Omeya in Damascus and the Azhar in Cairo.

Finally, if we want to look at the oldest doors of the mosque, we wust go to the **Puerta de San Estabán**; despite its bad corrosion, it is still the best example of this style of door during the Caliph period.

View of the Christian Cathedral inside the Mezquita.

Detail of the elaborate wooden choir-stalls.

A stirring view of the egg-shaped dome of the Crucero, whose splendour contrasts with the simplicity of the Arab building. ▶

ROMAN CORDOVA

The ancient patrician colony and capital city has left behind some interesting Roman monuments, together with famous figures like Seneca, the philosopher, the poet Lucan and the great Roman Christian figure of Bishop Osio, the rector of the Ecumenical Council of Nicea. The most important monument is the peaceful **bridge** which crosses the Guadalquivir in front of the mosque. It dates back to the times of Julius Caesar although it was touched up in later periods. The **bridge's doorway**, at the far end of the city, was erected during the reign of Philip V and its Herrenian, almost Classical, style goes well with the bridge's design. On the other end stands the **Torre de la Calahorra**; built by the Christians in the XVI century, it houses the **Historic Museum of the City**. Below we can still see remains of Arab windmills like the one of Albolafia, of Enmedio and the Molino de Papel. The image of the traditional Arab wheel used to extract water from the river is one of the typical pictures depicted in old coins and engravings.

Behind the Town Hall we can see fluted monumental columns with Corinthian capitals of a **Roman temple** which once stood there. There is little left of the Roman period, only wall fronts of this period and collections kept in the **Historical and Archaeological Museum** of the following item.

ALCAZAR DE LOS REYES CRISTIANOS

It is worth mentioning the Alcazar de los Cristianos, founded by Alfonso XI in the XVI century and where the Catholic Monarchs set up their court for a while. Within the walls, reinforced with towers, stands the old palace which is now a museum with some Roman sarcophagi and mosaics. Its evocative gardens seem to call back the Arab spirit, and the silent air, filled with the musicality of the fountains, seems to imitate echoes of Flamenco songs; the most important Flamenco festival is in fact held beside this enclosure every year.

◀ *The Roman bridge, with its sixteen arches spanning the river.*

◀ *On the right bank of the Guadalquivir, the Puerta del Puente, erected during the reign of Philip II in the shape of a triumphal arch in Doric style.*

Two images of the Alcazar of the Christian kings, with the statues of Isabelle, Ferdinand and Christopher Columbus.

The Moorish Puerta de Almodóvar, with the statue of
the philosopher Seneca born in Cordova.

Behind the statue of Averroës, who was born
in Cordova in 1126, stand the thick enclosing walls.

MOORISH AND JEWISH CORDOVA

We can also find wall fronts and various objects of
this period in the aforementioned Archaeological Museum. But the most important Arabic inheritance left in
the city is the mosque.

Besides this precious jewel, there is little left of the
original splendour of the city during the Caliph period.
The most outstanding remains are those of the city of
relaxation, the **Medina Azahara**, about a mile from the
urban city. This Caliph's «Versailles» was built in the X
century by Abderraman III, with a double wall, a defence system and a series of palaces and pavilions on
three terraces, excavated at the foot of the Sierra Morena; there was also a mosque, quarters, rooms, etc. and
an aqueduct to carry water from the mountains.

But this city was short-lived: after the fall of the Caliph, it was ransacked and destroyed only to be used centuries later as a quarry to obtain building materials. Thanks to excavations and reconstructions carried out for many years, we can now see the rebuilt «Royal room or room of the Viziers» and the mosque at an advanced stage of restoration. The museum in the enclosure of the Medina Azahara boasts a collection of various decorative pieces of stucco and and finely engraved marble.

The Jewish influence has also left its mark in Cordova. True Jewish art doesn't exactly exist as the Jews would usually adopt and make use of the prevailing art of every place and period. The remains in Cordova are strongly influenced by Islamic or Mudejar art. The **Jewish district** is one of the most typical and characteristic districts with its narrow side-streets and houses set in the walls, crammed with gardens, pools, and statues, next to the Puerta de Almodovar. There we come across the **Synagogue**, the only one preserved in Andalusia and dating back to the XIV century. Some Hebrew inscriptions are to be found on pieces of Arab style plasterwork. A simple statue of Maimonides commemorates the famous Jewish doctor and philosopher who filled Medieval culture with his knowledge.

In the heart of the Judería, the old Jewish ghetto, the small square and statue dedicated to the great Jewish thinker and doctor, Maimonides.

Plaza de los Dolores decorated by the statue of Cristo de los Faroles.

The Encarnación lane and the Patio Judería. ▶

SILENT CORDOVA

Another characteristic which adds to its charm is the silence that reigns over the city. When a poet defined Cordova as the silent city, it is because he walked through the peaceful and undisturbed patios and streets. A paradise of elegantly designed noble patios, lit up by the metallic reflection of the marble tiles, and of patios shining in the light of white lime, overflowing with flowers and geraniums, filled with a play on light and shadow around the pool epicentre.

Silent Cordova reveals its Arab influence through its prevailing perfume. In spring, the patios and side-streets are immersed in a pool of jazmine and orange-blossoms with a penetrating aroma of plants which is intensified over Easter with clouds of incense and burnt candle-wax. The streets of the silent city, a «deep wound cured with lime», are an important tourist attraction like its churches and museums. The **calleja de las flores**, de los Rincones de oro, de los Arquillos, de la Luna, Calle de la Hoguera, Calle Judios, Calle Comedias, the squares and street corners all form an enchanting world.

The Flamenco Festival, held every year, is one of its purest manifestations. As far as the art of bullfighting is concerned we just need to go to the **Museo de Arte Cordobés y Taurino**. Another similar museum is the small **Museo Julio Romero de Torres**. Unfortunately, works of great symbolic value are exhibited in distasteful backgrounds.

However, we discover more characteristic museums in the Cordovan squares and street-corners. In the **Plaza del Potro** is to be found one of the famous «*Triumphs*» dedicated to the archangel Raphael and a fountain quoted by Cervantes. Finally we come to the **Museo Provincial de Bellas Artes**, in the ancient hospital founded by the Catholic Monarchs. In this museum, next to great Spanish artists and some foreign artists there is also a small section dedicated to the artists of the city.

The Renaissance palace of Jeronimo Paez also houses the **Museo Arqueológico Provincial**, one of the most famous of its kind in Spain, not only for its resources but also for its complete musical conception and model setting. It features collections of prehistoric objects, Iberian, Roman and Palaeo-Christian antiques, as well as ceramics, statues, gold and silver works, stained-glass windows, etc. It also boasts some famous Islamic objects coming from the Medina Zahara.

◀ *Plaza del Potro referred to by Cervantes in* Don Quixote.

◀ *The façade of the church of S. Marina: in the square the monument to Manolete, the most famous spanish bullfighter.*

The church of S. Marina.

An example of workmanship on leather, typical craftsmanship of the city.

Parque Nacional Coto Doñana

The *Parque Nacional Coto Doñana*, source of pride to Andalusia, lies in the Southwest corner of Spain; the beauty of this nature park is outstanding, not only because of the various swamps and woods found here and there, but also for its setting along the coast, where candid dunes shift in the winds. Along the course of River Guadalquivir and as far as its estuary, deer and wild boars, shy lynxes and elegant fallow deer, rare golden eagles and delightful pink flamingos all have their habitat here, where the umbrella pines tower over thick carpets of shrubs. And during Winter, thousands of migrating birds find a sheltered haven in the almost 100,000 hectares of the park, attracted by the pleasant waters of the enormous swamps. Many years ago, the entire area was a popular game reserve (*coto*) belonging to a noble family. Then, in 1969, the whole territory was placed under naturalistic restrictions and was officially declared protected. Since then, flora and fauna have been able to reproduce unhindered, not at all disturbed by the occasional presence of humans: visits around the park are exclusively by appointment and only a few people at a time are allowed entrance.

Overview of the port and city. *An impressive view of the majestic Alcazaba.* ▶

ALMERIA

Almería can be described as the least visited, yet best known, part of Andalusia.

Few tourists make their way to this extremely dry corner of Spain, where only special crops are grown. It would be unusual to find tourists, who usually invade the Costa del Sol, lying on the wild, undisturbed beaches of this «dead corner». Here tradition is combined with avant-garde structures in the villages and urban developments like the Mojacar area. Few people are familiar with the craftmanship of this remote area, which is therefore still beautifully unspoilt. Yet millions of spectators have at one time or another seen its deserts and black, picturesque ravines, as the background for spaghetti westerns and other similar types of film.

Almería also has a rich history. Founded by the Phoenicians, it underwent a series of invasions and became one of the most important ports of the peninsula during the Omeyan emirate of Cordova. A popular saying which symbolizes its importance in the past goes «When Almería was Almería, Granada was only its *alqueria* or farmhouse».

But after the fall of the Cordovan Caliph and its moment of glory as the capital of an independent emirate, it fell to the Almohades in 1091, becoming a pirates' refuge. It was conquered by Alfonso VII in 1147, then it fell once more to the Arabs shortly afterwards. It was finally surrendered to the Catholic Monarchs in 1489 during their invincible campaign for the unification of the country under the sign of the cross.

The Arabic name Almería means «mirror», a fitting name if from a distance you look at the city resting on top of the hill with its proud golden castle rising up from its enclosure and reflected in the still green waters of the Mediterranean.

THE ALCAZABA

The castle is Almería's most attractive place to visit. Founded in the X century by the Cordovan Caliph, Abderraman III, it was later enlarged by Almanzor and then by Hayran, the first independant emir of Almería. It covers a rocky hill and, at the foot of the hill, the city sprawls, protected by many walls with battlements.

After crossing the first enclosure, which is now a garden, we come to the second enclosure where we find the emir's palace. Only the foundations of the baths and rooms of the palace still stand. In the third enclosure stands a defence bastion re-built by the Catholic Monarchs.

THE CATHEDRAL

Even the Cathedral has a fortress look about it. In fact the front defence walls of the enclosure which face the sea were reinforced. Work began at the beginning of 1524 according to designs by Diego de Siloé, but it was never completed. The most important *façade* is the one facing the Plaza de la Catedral. A Renaissance façade like the one in the Calle Perdones, both created by Juan de Orea in the XVI century. There are some interesting works of art in the dark and rather sombre interior of

◀ *A view of the battlemented walls of the old Arab fortress of Alcazaba.*

◀ *The classicizing portal to the left side of the Cathedral.*

This and following pages: four pictures of the district of Chanca, with its caves dug into the tufo.

the Cathedral. In the main chapel stands is a fine eighteenth-century altar-piece; in the choir, there are *choir-stalls* engraved by Juan de Orea, the same artist who painted the façades; the tomb of the Cathedral's founder, Bishop Villalan, is in one of the chapels together with the Flemish *Araoz altar-piece*; there are also two important eighteenth-century masterworks: *a Salzillo sculpture* and the neoclassical architecture behind the *choir*, by Ventura Rodriguez.

BARRIO DEL CHANCO

There are other important churches, like the ones of Santiago, San Pedro and Santo Domingo etc., and picturesque quarters like the Barrio del Chanco, but the most important part of the visit is the Sierra de Gador, via the Berja and Ugijar road, where one can admire the unique country-side or look for the dark ravines and dry rivers of the Almería desert; this faraway country of intrepid adventures is at times depicted in the magic of the cinema.

Panorama over the port of Malaga and over the green Paseo del Parque.

An aerial view of the Plaza de Toros in Malaga. ▶

MALAGA

A poet defined Malaga as a musical city, which pratically sums it up. A city of poets which gave birth to the Nobel prize winner, Vicente Aleixandre and to many of the 1927 Generation. It is a happy and confident city as capital of the Costa del Sol, an elegant and bustling coastline which competes with the traditional Italian and French Rivieras. Today, celebrities, the nobility and oil-sheiks come to take refuge in this paradise of fame, sun and golden beaches which also attracts legions of snow-white tourists who crowd together on charter planes from all over the world to mingle with the jet-set.

Malaga and the Costa del Sol welcome them one by one with their open character. This happy and musical city has been the land of exile for centuries. Every race has passed through it; its sweet and dense wine has been loaded on to Phoenician and Roman ships and its starry sky has comforted melancholic emirs, the same sky which now accompanies the tourists' clumsy Flamenco clapping in the taverns.

According to Strabo it was founded by the Phoeni-cians. It then fell to the Carthaginians and later to the Romans. In 711 it was taken by the Arabs and was made the capital of an independent emirate which did not give in to the Cordovan Abderraman's rule. After the Christian siege in 1487, it was taken over by the Catholic Monarchs, but many Moors continued to live there until they were expelled by Philip III at the beginning of the XVII century. Malaga played an important role during the fights between the Liberals and the Absolutists in the last century; General Riego proclaimed the Liberal Constitution here in 1820. Its monuments and urban developments suffered greatly. The same happened in 1931 after the proclamation of the Republic and the Civil War in 1936.

A city which has been invaded by all races, yet which has still maintained its musical and easy-going character. It is important not only for its relaxing beaches and «dolce far niente» but also for its industry and commerce. Its port is the most important in Andalusia and there are as many merchants as tourists ready to experience its ancient hospitality.

Overview of the Cathedral.

Above, one side of the Cathedral.

Right, the impressive façade. ▶

ROMANS, MOORS AND CHRISTIANS

On the two hills which overlook the welcoming port are some noble remains of the city's past. At the foot of the hill dominated by the castle lies the Roman theatre and the Gibralfaro Castle connected to the Alcazaba by its defence walls. At the foot of both hills are the Cathedral, the sanctuary and the city, filled with majestic processions over Easter.

THE CATHEDRAL

The same thing has happened to the Cathedral as to the Victory of Samothrace or to the broken busts of classical statues, that is to say, nobody can imagine the Cathedral ever being complete.

Nonetheless, it still looks magnificent. Work began in 1528, according to designs by Diego de Siloé, but was discontinued in 1783. A tower and part of the central pediment were left incomplete. However with the passing of time and force of habit, the great façade seems to have found a happy medium which no-one would ever dream of changing.

In the vast and elegant interior, we find some first class works, like the «*Pietà*» by Alonso Cano in the retrochoir, or the forty *statuettes of saints* by Pedro de Mena in the choir stalls. In the chapels, one can admire works by Alonso Cano, Mateo Cerezo, and Pedro de Mena which include *Saints and praying statues of the Catholic Monarchs.*

Another part of this incomplete structure is the Baroque façade of the Episcopal Palace opposite the cathedral. Further on, next to the gardens around the Cathedral, one comes across the **Sagrario** or sanctuary with its splendid Queen Isabel doorway and Plateresque *altarpiece* by Juan de Balmaseda inside.

Although Malaga isn't as picturesque as most Andalusian capitals, it makes up for its architectural weakness with its pleasant collection of avenues and parks, a paradise around the chaotic centre.

There are however some interesting churches and buildings, like the **circular Iglesia del Santo Cristo**; the **Consulate** built in 1782; the **Iglesia de San Pedro** and its small **Museum de la Semana Santa**; the **Iglesia de Santiago el Mayor**, one of the oldest churches, built in 1490 and which still has a pre-existing Mudejar tower; the church of **Nuestra Señora de la Victoria**, built by the Catholic Monarchs shortly after the seizure of the city, on the same spot where they had their Royal tent; inside there is a moving «Dolorosa» by Pedro de Mena.

A picture of the large Park of Malaga and the well groomed gardens in front of the Ayuntamiento, *the elegant Municipal Hall.*

Other churches have a more sentimental and romantic value, like the chapel dedicated to the popular legend of *Zamarrilla*, later described in literature. It is the strange story of a famous bandit who was caught by surprise with his lover by the police. He ran away and hid in the niche containing the statue of the Virgin. When the police entered the church, they looked in the niche but could not see anything; then the bandit, in appreciation, placed a carnation on the breast of the Virgin Mary but it began to bleed.

THE CASTLE OF GIBRALFARO

The castle's walls join it to the Alcazaba. It is a Phoenician fortress rebuilt by the Emir Yusuf in the XIV century. Although there is little to see, we can enjoy the view over the city and its parks around the piers of the port, over the «Malagueta» or the promenade which makes it well worth the climb.

THE ALCAZABA

On the same hill, we can see the castle, which was also a Roman fortress at one time, but it was rebuilt by the Moors in the IX century and the Governer's residence was set up there. For many centuries this enclosure was greatly neglected but after persistent restoration, it regained the pureness of its original form and gardens. One of the pavilions next to the Granada door houses a small **Archaeological Museum** containing prehistorical, Roman, Visigothic and Arab collections; the most outstanding pieces are Roman statues and some Hispo-Muslem ceramics.

The thick walls of the Gibralfaro form a backdrop for a charming fountain.

The sober gardens which soften the rough, powerful lines of the Alcazaba.

COSTA DEL SOL

The beautiful, sun-blessed Costa del Sol, the ancient land of Andalusian fishermen now an authentic paradise for Spanish and international tourism, stretches out where bright blue skies blend into the turquoise, crystal-clear sea, between Granada and the Strait of Gibraltar. All along the continuous strip of white sands that winds its way through the creeks and inlets of southern Andalusia, a picturesque succession of attractive seaside resorts has developed in the shade of the orange-groves: **Motril**, modern and lively; delightful **Almuñécar**; **Nerja**, famous for the enchanted atmosphere of its caves full of stalactites and stalagmites; **Torremolinos**, which developed rapidly out of an old fishing village, chaotic, full of long avenues, hotels, entertainment and particularly popular facilities for tourists; then there is quieter **Fuengirola**; and **Marbella,** a city with an age-old centre, capital of fashionable, aristocratic, luxury tourism, sufficiently sumptuous to be the spot preferred by millionaires and film stars; or **Estepona**, quiet and on a human scale; **Sotogrande**, more exclusive and elite.

All the tourists who come here, whether wealthy or not, can rest assured that no matter which resort they have chosen, the sea will always be splendid and inviting, the sky will always be clear, the facilities will be modern and top quality, and the beaches will be spacious and well-equipped. Not to mention the typical little harbours where numerous sports craft berth; or the characteristic restaurants where delicious seafood is served accompanied by the unmistakable wines of the South; the fashionable places that make night-life lively and irresistible; and the 30 or more lush-green, golf courses, for a sport that is becoming more and more popular here. And, for those who want a little bit more than just sunshine and a host of water sports, what could be better than a relaxing trip inland, to see some of the most beautiful places in Andalusia, the typical white-washed villages that stand out on the slopes of the Sierra and that have won the hearts of poets and artists through the ages, from **Mijas** to **Casares**, and **Gaucín**.

Typical scenery along the Costa del Sol and, above, the splendid golf courses; following pages: sun-drenched beaches, charming little harbours, well-appointed hotels and transparent, calm seas are found in every corner.

Above, a picture of Benalmádena-Costa.

◄ Nerja, the enchanting beach of Calahonda.

◄ Mijas: the village and a "Burro-Taxi" (lit. donkey-taxi).

Sun-kissed beaches of Marbella (above) and Estepona (left).

113

BAEZA
JAÉN
ÚBEDA

The picturesque Andalusian country-side is scattered here and there with pleasant towns that contain real architectural treasures: two of these towns are Baeza and Úbeda, splendid examples of Spanish Renaissance near the *Sierra de Cazorla* – a magnificent nature park –, incredibly rich in history and majestic monuments, like the ancient *churches* in Úbeda and the great *palaces* in Baeza. But this can also be said of Jaén, near the border between Andalusia and Castile, once a compulsory stop for caravans and now a town with spectacular buildings (the most beautiful is the XVI century **Cathedral**) watched over by the menacing **Castillo de Santa Catalina**, a fortress erected by Ferdinand III in 1246 over the spot of a previous Moorish stronghold.

Above, the Fuente de Santa María (1564) in Baeza, on front of the Seminary, designed by the architect Ginés Martínez to resemble a triumphal arch; on the left, the monumental Jaén Cathedral; below, the doorway of the Iglesia de San Pablo, in Úbeda.

Ronda, with the stunning Puente Nuevo, dominates the valley from its rocky spur. Right: the Philip V Arch.

On the following pages: the Plaza de Toros and one of the paintings Goya dedicated to bull-fighting.

RONDA

Perched high on a rock and surrounded by cliffs, divided into two parts by a 90 metre deep gorge bridged by the monumental, XIX century **Puente Nuevo,** the white-washed town of Ronda that was impregnable for many centuries and was not returned to Christendom until 1485, is an interesting place because of the remains of a Roman Theatre, its white Moorish houses, Arabian baths, splendid palaces, an elegant *Town Hall* and, above all, its grand **Plaza de Toros,** one of the oldest in Spain (1785) and the birth-place of modern bull-fighting. In fact, this was the realm of the legendary torero called Pedro Romero, who was responsible for the 'Ronda' style still in use. In September every year, one of the most popular events in the whole country is held here. The town has an interesting **Bull Museum** dedicated to the art of bull fighting and where there are even prints by Goya representing scenes in the bullring.

*"The bull is the greatest poetical
and spiritual treasure belonging to Spain"*
Federico García Lorca

The bull-fight

Bull-fighting, which descends from ancient
tauromachy, was a pastime for aristocrats for a long
time until the XVIII century, when the Bourbons and
legendary toreros like Pedro Romero and Pepe-Hillo
transformed it into an incredibly popular and
spectacular performance. Nowadays, every Spanish
city, whether large or small, has its own bullring (plaza
de toros), and the relative programme of bullfights is
often linked with the festivities for their Patron Saints.
Hence, at five o'clock in the afternoon, three toreros
(matadores) enter the bullring, each with two
picadores (toreros on horseback) and three
banderilleros at his side, and each with two bulls to
fight. Before a crowd of exited, eager spectators, this
age-old challenge is repeated and braved with solemn
ritual and with the enthusiasm of a work of art. The
matador performs a series of traditional passes with
his cape to joust the bull, and then he 'hands it over'
to the picadores whose task is to tire it. Next come the
banderilleros, who tackle the bull and stab it with
their banderillas decorated with ribbons. However, it
is the matador who comes back into the scene to kill
the bull: armed with his sword and muleta, the
famous red cape, he fells it with a single, well-aimed
thrust. When the performance has been particularly
enthralling, the spectators roar their enthusiasm and
the matador is awarded the bull's ear as a trophy.

CADIZ

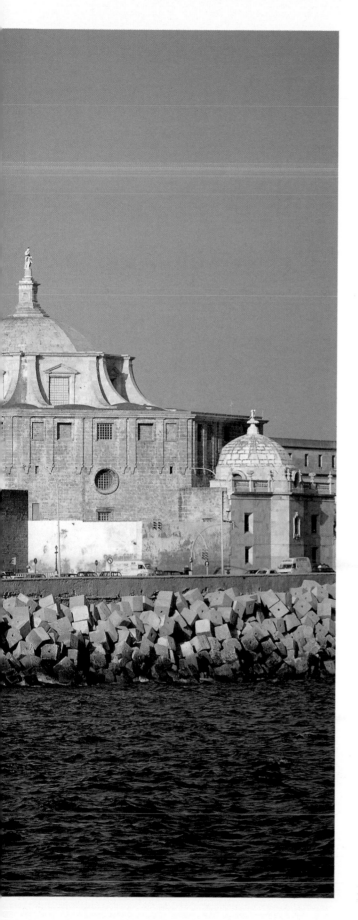

Cadiz is a seaside town built on the edge of an isthmus and surrounded by a bright silver bay; it is now closed off by a road-bridge which avoids going all the way round.

The sea has always played an important role in its history. Cadiz is one of the oldest cities in the west, where trading between the Phoenician ports of Tyre and Sidon took place as far back as the XII century. The Bible describes this trading with the Phoenician ships which took away manufactured products in exchange for bronze and silver.

The Phoenician Gadir became Carthaginian and then the Roman Gades. It later fell to the Arab invaders after the battle of Guadalete in 711 and was finally conquered by Alfonso X in 1262.

After the discovery of America, its port became very important as it was besieged by the English. During the War of Independence, it was the final place of refuge for the liberals who met in the Cortes and proclaimed the famous Constitution of 1812, which was later abolished by Ferdinand III's Absolutism, although it still preserved the strength of a symbol and ideal.

Today Cadiz is a great transatlantic port, with ships sailing regularly to Barcelona, the Canary Islands and South America.

It is a restless social and cultural city with important tourist resources around the actual city and province. The names of the villages remind us of the problematic «frontera» fought over for centuries by Christians and Muslems.

There are not many ancient relics to see in the city itself, as many were destroyed in wars, especially during the riots of the last century. We have to go to the **Archaeological Museum** to see some native Turdetanos, Phoenician and Carthaginian relics. However Cadiz has never been excavated systematically and new remains are discovered when building new structures.

The Cathedral of Cadiz is late XVIII century, and

The Cathedral of Cadiz seen from the sea.

121

only when one looks at it from the sea does it lose its heavy Baroque and Neoclassic style. Inside, the choir-stalls by Pedro Duque Cornejo are interesting to see. There are also some important statues, like *St. Bruno* by Montañés or the *Crucifix* attributed to Alonso Cano, together with some paintings like the «*Inmaculada*» by Murillo and the treasured «*Custodia del Millón*» by Arfe.

In the **Oratory of San Felipe Neri**, where the Cortes met to plan the Constitution of 1812 during the French siege, there is a famous *Inmaculada* by Murillo on the main altar. We can discover many pieces in other churches and chapels which add colour and variation to the city. We can visit the old cathedral, founded in the XIII century and rebuilt in the XVII century, or the *Chapel of the Hospital del Carmen*, with an admirable Greco and a passageway of XVIII century enamel tiles. There is the *Iglesia de la Santa Cueva* with some wall paintings by Goya; the **Iglesia de San Augustin** with *sculptures* by Martinez Montañés; the **Capilla de Santa Catalina** on the outer road of the peninsula facing the sea with paintings by Murillo on the high altar including his last work during the completion of which he fell from the scaffolding and killed himself, and sculptures by the Murcian Salzillo.

The city's best artistic treasures are to be found in the **Museum of Fine Arts** which is one of the richest and most interesting art galleries in the Andalusian region. There are various works by Murillo, Ribera, Alonso Cano, Rizi, Carreno, Claudio Coello etc. The museum also features works by foreign artists, like Rubens or Van Eyck. But its most outstanding collection is the *Zurbaran's Collection* which has some of the best examples of Zurbaran art which come from the once prosperous but now abandoned Carthusian Monastery of Jerez.

One of the numerous beaches around Cadiz.

The solemn Colegiata, source of pride of Jerez architecture and, below, a modern azulejo with a religious theme.

JEREZ AND ARCOS
DE LA FRONTERA

Jerez de la Frontera is another Andalusian village characterized by its own special myth. While in Ronda it was the bullfighting, here it is the famous «Carthusian» horses and its famous sherry.

Its art entwines itself around Andalusian mythology. Its magnificent Collegiate church acts as the setting for the popular annual wine-harvest festivals. The monastery is only a few kilometres away from the centre, with its Gothic cloister; it was where the famous Carthusian horses were kept, and is where the annual fair is held. There are many artistic, religious and civil treasures, like the remains of the castle, Arab baths, towers and walls, convents, churches, palaces etc. There are also some peculiar cathedrals: the so-called «wine cathedrals» which are huge cellars where different types of sherry are made using a strange, traditional method.

123

Two pictures of the Colegiata
at Jerez de la Frontera.

Arcos de la Frontera has its own distinctive character, filled with monuments and works of art, like the
castle, town hall, churches, convents, chapels, hospitals,
etc. Yet what makes it special is the actual layout of the
village, with groups of houses and side-streets leading
up to the church and to the look-out of the Castle of the
Dukes of Arcos. An unforgettable scene used as the setting for the most characteristic Easter processions and
which inspired many famous stories from Spanish literature and music like the «wicked miller» and the «love-
sick magistrate».

There are even more picturesque villages: **Vejer de la
Frontera**, with its Arab castle dominating the Moorish
settlement, making it one of the most typical villages in
the coast; **Castellar de la Frontera**, a prototype of the
«white villages» of the mountain range, with its castle
over the straits of Gibraltar; Jimena de la Frontera, Co-
nil de la Frontera, Chiclana de la Frontera, etc.

BEHIND *SHERRY*

The procedure employed to produce an excellent *Sherry* entails many steps that have been handed down throughout the centuries and which are followed almost like a solemn ritual. The Jerez wine is made from *Palomino* and *Pedro Ximénez* grapes proportionately mixed according to the desired strength. The grapes are harvested during the first half of September: the *Palomino* grapes are submitted immediately to pressing, while long straw mats await the *Pedro Ximénez* ones that have to dry out in the sun so that the sugar-content can reach its highest concentration. Pressing is carried out in cylindrical tanks, generally during the night when it is cooler. The liquid then flows out into the fermentation tanks. The next step foresees filling the casks, placed one on top of another in a pyramid: the ones highest up, the younger ones, are for the new wine, which will then be blended with the older wine contained in the casks further down the pyramid.

This system, known as *solera*, guarantees constant quality. The degree of alcohol

(between 15° and 18°) is adjusted by adding wine spirit. The last step consists in bottling the wine, which is drawn exclusively from the bottom casks containing the oldest wine: then the *Sherry* is ready to set out and conquer the world.

On the following pages: the flow of the tranquil Guadalete creates wide bends in the endless alluvial plains in Andalusia, like a peaceful snake wandering through cultivated land, a land made particularly fertile by waters from its floods.

INDEX